PESSIMISM, QUIETISM
AND NATURE AS REFUGE

PESSIMISM, QUIETISM AND NATURE AS REFUGE

David E. Cooper

agenda
publishing

First published in 2024 by Agenda Publishing

Agenda Publishing Limited
PO Box 185
Newcastle upon Tyne
NE20 2DH

www.agendapub.com

ISBN 978-1-78821-769-9 (hardcover)
ISBN 978-1-78821-770-5 (paperback)

British Library Cataloguing-in-Publication Data
A catalogue record for this book is available
from the British Library

Typeset in Nocturne by Patty Rennie

Printed and bound in the UK by
CPI Group (UK) Ltd, Croydon, CR0 4YY

Contents

Acknowledgements

I am grateful to Steven Gerrard for his meticulous and helpful copy-editing. My thanks also go to John Shand for his comments, both sympathetic and critical, on a draft of this book. I am especially grateful to Ian James Kidd not only for his detailed observations on each draft chapter, but for correspondence and discussions over several years on the themes addressed in my book.

Prologue

The man was returning, after a gap of thirty years, to the landscape in which, as a teenage boy, he loved to wander. He could remember clearly the forest of Scots pine and birch through which he would walk almost every day and, beyond its fringe, the fast-running river that joined the loch to the sea. He could still picture the hillside that rose from the opposite bank of the river: amongst the heathers and bracken, he would, on clear days, see deer, fox, rabbits, even weasels and badgers – all of them under the watchful eyes of the red kites that circled above.

Three decades on the place was very different. The forest had gone: only the stumps of the trees remained, jutting from muddy soil criss-crossed by bulldozer tracks. The river no longer tumbled, but flowed languidly, towards the sea, its surface covered with scum from a salmon farm built further up the loch. On the hillside beyond, the heathers and bracken had disappeared, burnt by fires resulting from the freak temperatures of the summer. There would, the man knew, be no deer, foxes or rabbits inhabiting this desert. Most of them would anyway have become victims of the shooters who, in recent years, paid large sums of money to kill almost anything that moved. The red kites, with no animals to keep an eye on, had flown elsewhere.

As he looked at this devastated environment, the man fought to suppress the animosity, hatred even, that he started to feel towards humankind. The desolation before him was, after all, down to human beings, not "the forces of nature". This was so even with the heathland fires, which registered humanly engineered climate change. Nor were the interventions responsible for the desolation the result of honest mistakes or of benign intentions gone awry. Instead they manifested human failings: greed, hubris, cruelty, indifference, mindlessness, and many others.

Incipient feelings of hatred towards human beings were not new to the man. Whether on his travels, through watching television documentaries, or reading about the fate of species and environments, he had encountered many other instances of human depredation of the natural world. The images remained with him: columns of dust-covered elephants in a vain search for water, once-virgin moorlands now pockmarked with wind turbines, fish struggling to breathe in polluted rivers, birds crippled by black oil, floating islands of plastic waste in estuaries, pheasants bred to be shot but instead squashed by cars. The pictures that floated before him might have come from an illustrated catalogue of the products of human avarice, ignorance and callousness.

Typically, he shook off these feelings. Hatred, after all, was one of the serious human failings complicit in the activities that aroused these hostile feelings. There was something else, however – something more abiding – that the man had no desire to shake off. This was a considered, reflective and very negative judgement on the moral or spiritual condition of humankind. He had no wish to reject or ignore a judgement whose truth, over the years, had become more and more obvious to him. Nor did he want to ignore certain moods, uncomfortable though they were, appropriate to this judgement – moods experienced by anyone who is serious in their negative appraisal of humankind.

The man I have been describing, with only some poetic licence, is real enough. But he could be anyone – anyone, that is, whose experience of humankind's treatment of animals, oceans, landscapes and forests has led them, like him, to a dark, negative verdict on humankind. I suspect that many of those reading this book identify with this man, for the question it addresses concerns the appropriate response to his verdict. The reader of the book is intended to ask, like its author, "How, if at all, should I adjust, shape and conduct my life in the light of this negative appraisal of the human condition?"

It is important to stress the first-personal form of this question. Moral debate about environmental issues is usually, and regrettably, dominated by questions about how "we" should act, think and feel. Here, "we" loosely refers to people in general, to people collectively, to society. These questions typically get answered by demanding that we reduce our consumption of material goods, drive and fly less, have fewer children, redistribute wealth to poorer countries, curb free-market capitalism, and so on.

Perhaps these are sensible answers, in the sense that if people at large did the things demanded, depredation of the earth could be slowed and even brought to an end. But they are not answers that have any clear relevance to how I, in particular, should respond to my negative verdict on humankind. For a start, the things that are demanded of us may strike me as pie in the sky. What bearing on my life has the proposal radically to reduce consumption when I know that this won't happen? I may think that it is already too late for us to do anything of a radical kind to redress the situation, but I still need to ask myself how I should conduct my life. For another thing, even if something that we might collectively do is both desirable and feasible, I may know that my contribution to this collective effort is vanishingly small. If so, aren't there more worthwhile, and more effective, things I should be doing with my life?

So you should be asking yourself, "How should *I* respond to my negative assessment of the human condition?", fully aware that your question cannot be settled by speculating on whether something would be "a good thing" if we – people in general – were to aim for it. In asking this question, you accord with the wisdom of the ancient Greeks, who recognized that "the point of entry for ethical reflection" is the good of your life as a whole.[1] A failure to address this question is just that – a failure: an evasion of a responsibility to examine your own life.

It is the question I'll be addressing to myself in this book, in the hope that my reflections on it may prove helpful to others. I'll be developing a line of thought that takes us from a pessimistic perception of the human condition to, eventually, the cultivation of what some might regard as a religious sensibility. It will travel through a recommendation of a quietist stance towards the human world and a recognition of a need for refuge from that world.

There is no inexorable logic to this line of thought. Any request for a proof of the best way to live in response to the negative verdict on humankind would be misplaced. But it is a cogent line of thought and one that traces a path on which many people, I hope, will want to travel. It is a line that defines a way of reflection, emotion, mood and comportment towards

the world that offers a certain peace to the anxieties and concerns to which the pessimistic verdict gives rise.

The man described at the beginning of this prologue might,
instead of being a traveller in a ruined landscape, have been a
journalist in war-torn areas, a social worker in crime-ridden
slums, or a doctor trying to save the victims of religious
persecution. He may, that is, have been a direct witness to
"man's inhumanity to man", as Robert Burns called it,[2] and it
may have been this, rather than our depredation of the non-
human world, that confirmed for him a negative judgement of
humankind. Or, as with Burns himself, it may have been all of
this – our treatment of each other, of animals, and of the land
– that secured the man's pessimistic verdict.

So, why do I draw attention in the first instance, not to
inhumanity to man, but to the devastation of the natural
world? Well, for a start, this attention is not narrow or exclusive: many of the human failings that invite the negative
verdict are on display in the treatment of human beings and
nature alike. Reflection on the travails of a natural world under
the dominion of human beings is not, therefore, to ignore
the plight of men and women who suffer from domination
and exploitation as well. Indeed, it is a plight that sometimes
resembles that of the animals that suffer at our hands. Much
of what I shall say about quietism, refuge and religious sensibility does not specifically depend on my starting point – the
depredation of the natural world.

Second, it is my impression that, these days, it is a pessimistic perception based on our treatment of nature to which
voice is most loudly given. Pronouncements on the greed,
rapaciousness and callousness of human beings are, I find,
most likely to be heard in the context of environmental discussions. In part, perhaps, this recent concentration results

from recognition that some human failings are at their most salient – their most "pure" – in our treatment of animals and natural environments. There are failings – hubris, for example – that might be overlooked or given insufficient prominence in a catalogue of vices compiled on the basis of inhumanity to man. But they can hardly be ignored in connection with our treatment of nature.

Finally, it is an important claim made later in this book that nature – natural environments and their occupants – is the most promising place in which to seek a kind of refuge from the all-too-human world that invites a pessimistic verdict. It seems sensible, therefore, that people's relationship with the natural world should, from its beginning, have been a prominent subject of the book's attention.

1

The human condition

The dark reckoning of the human condition by the man we encountered in the Prologue had several sources – first-hand experience, documentaries and newspaper reports, but also works of philosophy and religion. Experience and the documentaries confirmed claims he had studied in these works, while they in turn helped him to articulate what he saw on his travels or watched on his computer screen. No work had done this more effectively than the recorded teachings of a man who lived two and a half millennia earlier – Siddhattha Gotama, familiarly known as the Buddha.

Not only did the Buddha express a deeply negative judgement on humankind, but he provided what perhaps remains the most detailed and penetrating account of its moral and spiritual failings. This book, incidentally, is not intended to be a study of Buddhism, and I do not write as a card-carrying Buddhist, but at several points I draw upon the insights to be found in the discourses of the Buddha. In the Prologue I briefly described the line of thought that this book will follow, and it

1

is no accident if, at some stages, this line coincides with the path taught by the Buddha.

In his first discourse after the night of his enlightenment, the Buddha formulated the four famous "noble truths".[1] The first two are "the truth of suffering" and "the truth of the origin of suffering". When unpacked, these terse pronouncements articulate the Buddha's dark vision of humankind. Suffering (*dukkha*) should be understood in a broad way: it comprises not only the physical pains of illness, injury and approaching death but failure to get the things we most want and encounters with those to which we are most averse. Indeed, suffering is the lot of any creatures, like ourselves, that are "aggregates" of body, feeling, perception, desire and consciousness. Frustration at failure, anxiety concerning the future, envy of those who get what they want, addiction and remorse – these, too, are forms of suffering. Even in the case of illness and approaching death, the Buddha's focus is less on physical pain than on the fear, resentment, anxiety, or disappointments that these invite.

The emphasis on attitudes, moods and perceptions helps explain the claim of the second noble truth that the origin of suffering is "craving" (*tanha* – literally "thirst"). This, too, requires unpacking. "Craving" or "greed" (*lobha*) refers, unsurprisingly, to sensual, especially sexual, desire, to gluttony, and to the unconstrained pursuit of material goods. But the term also embraces jealousy and envy, over-ambition, the pursuit of status and fame. It covers, indeed, all those desires and aims that betray the extent and depth of people's sense of self-importance, of their urge to organize the world for the sake of their own self-satisfaction.

Greed, the Buddha explains, combines with hatred and culpable ignorance or delusion to form the three "unwholesome roots" of human failings. They are not, however, independent of one another and greed or craving remains a central cause of suffering. Our self-centred desires inspire hatred of those who are better off than ourselves – hatred that makes it all too easy to become the victims of convenient delusions about them: delusions that, in turn, reinforce hatred and the desire to prosper at their expense.

This is just one of many examples in the Buddha's discourses of a dynamic and mutually reinforcing process that governs our failings. Another important one is this: our desires cause us to go in pursuit of gain, which then results in attachment to what we procure – an attachment that soon turns into a defensive possessiveness that sets us against one another. "The taking up of ... weapons, conflicts, quarrels, insults and slander, and falsehood" are the outcome.[2]

As this example shows, suffering is not confined to the unfortunate results for individuals of their desires or greed. It suffuses our relationships with one another: the suffering my unsatisfied desires cause me leads me to try harder to satisfy them and to be envious of others' success. The suffering I then impose on others in pursuit of my aims causes conflicts that make my situation worse, which then drives me to a more frenetic pursuit of these aims ... and so the cycle continues.

For the Buddha, in fact, the very structures of human existence guarantee that its character is one of suffering. What "keeps the [human] world turning around" are "eight worldly conditions" (*lokadhamma*), that include people's preoccupations with gain and loss, fame and disrepute, and praise and blame. It is an obsession with these that shapes social intercourse and our dealings with the world. This, and our other cravings, are why, he warns, everything is "burning", so that the human world is on balance one of "dejection and despair".[3]

3

BUDDHISM, PESSIMISM AND MISANTHROPY

The first two noble truths are, in effect, wonderfully abbreviated declarations of pessimism and misanthropy, when these terms are understood, not in their popular senses, but in those they have acquired in philosophical discussion.[4] They are to be understood as appraisals of humankind, not as feelings – even though certain moods and emotions are inevitably invited by the appraisals. Pessimism, in the relevant sense, is not a gloomy, jaded feeling, but a judgement – or, rather, a pair of judgements. First of all, for the philosophical pessimist, the human condition is a bad one: pain, suffering, anxiety, disappointment and unhappiness outweigh their opposites. Second, it is a condition that is very unlikely substantially to improve: indeed, it is one that has likely worsened with the development of modern civilization. There are, after all, far more people than there once were to suffer through starvation, warfare, pandemics, oppression, disappointment and anxiety.

Misanthropy, as philosophers typically understand it these days, is not hatred of human beings but a negative judgement on the moral and spiritual condition of humankind, like the judgement passed by the man in the Prologue. Misanthropy, as one of its famous advocates, Jonathan Swift, remarked, is not directed at "John, Peter [and] Thomas", whom one may "heartily love", but at "that animal called man".[5] For the misanthrope, a salient, deep and ubiquitous mark of "that animal" is humankind's moral failings: greed, deception, envy, hubris, *amour-propre* and so on.

Pessimism and misanthropy are not the same and can be prised apart. There are, for example, misanthropes who, while harsh in their condemnation of humankind, think that

4

salvation is just around the corner. A god, the communist revolution, a scientific miracle, or whatever will bring about a transformation of humankind, thereby bringing to an end both suffering and evil. But, generally, pessimism and misanthropy are paired, with each lending support to the other. The sufferings, disappointments and anxieties identified by the pessimist serve to consolidate and exacerbate the failings exposed by the misanthrope. In turn, some of these failings make any radical melioration of our condition improbable. A society marked by selfishness, avarice, and obsession with status and material gain does not have the moral resources to reform itself. After all, if the misanthrope is right, the bad condition humankind finds itself in is not the result of passing and correctable circumstances – of, say, economic mismanagement and political blundering – but of entrenched human failings. Our sorry condition is down to how we are.

The Buddha, in making his indictment, is not content simply to list a huge number of human failings, ranging from envy, conceit and self-delusion to meanness, cruelty and treachery. As is suggested by the many names given to these failings – "cankers", "taints", "imperfections", "defilements", "perversions" and others – he is also a taxonomist. The failings in each group belong to the various ways in which they stand in the way of enlightenment and liberation from the baleful condition of humankind. It is worth noting that some failings might, these days, be classified as "intellectual" or "cognitive" rather than "moral" – a proclivity to adopt "wrong views", for example, or distorted perceptions of the world. But it's equally important to note that, for the Buddha, these kinds of failings reinforce one another. As we saw earlier, hatred of other people breeds deluded beliefs about them that then serve to intensify the hatred.

Of great significance, too, is the Buddha's exposure of a fundamental feature of human existence that disposes us to our many failings. Put simply, this is self-consciousness – not in the sense of mere self-recognition (of which many animals, too, are capable), but consciousness of being a person whose existence stretches back and forward in time. To be self-conscious, in this sense, is to recognize oneself as, say, the person who moved to Rome ten years ago, will be retiring from work next week, and will one day die.

This sense of oneself as an enduring person is not in itself toxic, but it spawns attitudes that may easily become so. Only creatures with this sense can have long-term goals, purposes and ambitions, and hence become possessive, greedy and brutal in pursuit of them. Only for such creatures can their lives be matters of reflective concern and interest – and so give scope for self-absorption, self-deception and narcissism. Only they can compare themselves with other selves – and so become envious, conceited, self-important, hateful and domineering. Only they, finally, can also experience uncertainty that their futures will turn out as they desire – and so suffer from angst and the restlessness and desperation that impel attempts to secure these futures.

Even supposedly "basic" or "animal" desires, like sexual desire, are inflected by these aspects of self-consciousness, and in effect cease to be merely "animal" ones. Sexual desire, in human beings, is not a simple urge, but a component in a network of desire that involves jealousy, possessiveness, domination and vanity. More generally, it is consciousness of self that gives the stamp to ordinary human existence, guaranteeing that it will revolve around the "worldly conditions" referred to earlier. Our form of life, that is, is marked by relentless pursuit of future gain, pleasure, reputation and praise – and by anxiety and fear that these goals are not attainable.

For the Buddha, consciousness of self not only enables and fosters this pursuit, its accompanying anxieties, and consequent suffering and moral failings, it is also, in a sense, a delusion. The doctrine of "not-self" (*anatta*) is best understood, not as an exercise in metaphysics – as a claim about what entities really exist – but as a correction to closely related mistakes we make about ourselves. One such mistake is to exaggerate how continuous and stable our lives are. I wrongly take for granted that my present desires, beliefs, tastes and so on will endure into the indefinite future. It is only because I do that I become so attached to – and "cling" to – things, projects and other people. Were I to appreciate that I, like everything else, is "impermanent", subject to change and contingency, these cravings and clingings would dissipate.

Another mistake is that people exaggerate their self-mastery, their capacity to order and control their lives and futures. This "pilot of my ship" delusion is complicit in greed, possessiveness and other ills, for my relentless pursuit of fame, wealth and so on makes little sense if I am fully aware of fragility, change, and indeed of what I myself am. A person or self is not, as fondly imagined, this controlling pilot of a ship, but a complex process of interlocking and ever-changing feelings, beliefs, motives, bodily states and other "aggregates" (*khandas*). And this person exists in a world where everything and everyone is subject to conditions over which each of us has only very limited or no control.

Finally, the discourses of the Buddha indicate an explanation of why most people do not perceive the scale of suffering and moral failings. An explanation of this is important in order to answer the charge that, if pessimists and misanthropes are right, how is it that their judgements on humankind are not generally shared. For the Buddha, reluctance to endorse these judgements is primarily due to "ignorance" (*avijja*). By this, he does not mean ordinary, everyday lack of knowledge – although this, too, plays a role. Today, for example, people are surprisingly ignorant of the scale of suffering and depredation for which human beings are responsible – starvation, infant mortality, the destruction of animal habitats, and so on.

By "ignorance", however, the Buddha intends a failure to understand important general truths about the world and ourselves, including the impermanence of things, the nature of our own selves, the ubiquity of suffering, and the extent of our "impurities". Crucially, he argues that this ignorance is motivated. These are truths that would not be welcomed by people, bent as they are on the pursuit of pleasure, security and material gain. These are pursuits, with the consequent vices they encourage, that distort our perception of things and people: the ugly and impure, for instance, get seen as beautiful and pure when they accord with our desires. Or they incline us to "wrong views" – convenient fictions – that obstruct a clear view of things.[6] It is an interesting feature, moreover, of many of our failings – such as vanity and self-deception – that they serve to disguise our failings, including themselves. A person's immodesty, for instance, conceals from them their lack of modesty.

A BRIEF HISTORY OF PESSIMISM

The Buddha was not, of course, the only ancient thinker to express a pessimistic and misanthropic view of humankind. Indeed, in the India of his time, this seems to have been the default view, certainly among the ascetic teachers from whom he learnt, but also more widely among Brahmins and Jains. The question addressed by his contemporaries was not whether the human condition was a bad one, but how to extricate oneself from it. Further east, in China, his near contemporary, Confucius, came to despair of reversing the moral decline into which human beings had fallen. Two centuries later, the Daoist sage, Zhuangzi, emphasized, like the Buddha, how people had become "submerged" in a culture of restless acquisition and accumulation. They had abandoned the Way (*dao*) that alone leads to peace, harmony and happiness.

There were pronounced streaks of pessimism and misanthropy among the ancient Greeks, too. In the famous lines declaimed by the Chorus in Sophocles' *Oedipus at Colonos*, "never to have been born is best... and a close second is a quick return to where you came from". In the human world "murder, hatred, strife, resentment and envy" prevail, and there is only friendless "bitter old age" to look forward to.[7] Inherited from this dark outlook, and given a theological basis, the pronouncements of the early Christian Church Fathers were equally negative. The human condition is an "ill" one, said Tertullian, but thoroughly "deserved at God's hand", given the emergence, since the Fall, of "all vices and crimes".[8] For Augustine, too, "the misery of the human condition" is guaranteed by our "concupiscence" or "uncontrolled desire", also our lot since the Fall.[9]

It is easy to forget, in the climate of today's cheery, bright-siding Christian messages, that this negative judgement on humankind has always had its champions in the Church – Luther, Calvin and Kierkegaard, for example. In the face of this modern tendency, it is helpful to be reminded that, for Christianity – and the other Abrahamic religions

9

– "the central elements of the characteristically human form of life" were long perceived to be "self-love and false righteousness".[10]

By no means all later pessimists and misanthropes have rested their case on religious grounds. For Michel de Montaigne, in the sixteenth century, our troubles and failings owe to an absurd overestimation of our capacity to acquire understanding and to our febrile restlessness. A comparison of humankind with the animal kingdom shows we are quite wrong to place ourselves above the beasts in the moral hierarchy. For Thomas Hobbes, in the following century, people's indelible egoism makes their condition one of a potential "war of all against all" that only submission to a ruler with an iron hand can avert.

Selfishness and its terrible results remained an important emphasis of critics of humankind, with the best of them recognizing, as had the Buddha, that egoism is a uniquely human attribute. For Rousseau, the "depraved" condition of "civilised man" is due, above all, to *amour-propre*, the self-love or vanity that results from placing oneself above others and that "triggers all the evil men do".[11] For the Italian poet, Giacomo Leopardi, "egoism, envy and hatred" guarantee that "the world is the enemy of the good". But it was people's inevitable failure to achieve the happiness that their nature impels them to look for that confirms the poet's pessimism.[12] Leopardi's nineteenth-century admirers continued this theme. Arthur Schopenhauer, who wrote that "existence is a mistake", argues that the structure of desire ensures our suffering: for we constantly veer between the frustration of unsatisfied desires and the boredom that results when they are satisfied.[13] For Eduard von Hartmann, equally, "positive happiness" is "impossible": the remaining alternatives are "misery" and the "painlessness" finally achievable only through humankind's collective suicide.[14]

It is the fleeting character of our enjoyments and the long periods of deep boredom in-between that, for the acerbic Romanian-born twentieth-century misanthrope, Emil Cioran, entail that the human being is a "perpetually dissatisfied animal" – always ready to lash out, in frustration, at its fellows.[15] More recently, and in more measured prose than Cioran's, the South African philosopher, David Benatar, recalling the words of Sophocles' Chorus, has argued that it is "better never to have been". The quality of most lives is much worse than people imagine, and the enormous harms to one another, to animals and to the environment that human beings inflict provide, Benatar writes, "a misanthropic argument" for regarding "humanity [as] a moral disaster".[16]

Benatar is one of many contemporary authors to include harm to natural environments in an indictment of humankind. For some of these, indeed, this is at the very centre of their charge, thereby inviting the label "eco-misanthropists". While, unsurprisingly, eco-misanthropy is a recent phenomenon, there have always been thinkers troubled by people's exploitative and hubristic attitude towards nature. Around 300 BCE, the Daoist sage, Zhuangzi, was complaining that new-fangled methods in agriculture and husbandry threatened to spoil a simple and natural relationship with the land and animals.[17] "Romantic ecologists", like Wordsworth and Coleridge, feared for the fate of landscapes through industrial expansion, including the building of railways. Similar fears for the integrity of wilderness permeated the writings of Emerson, Thoreau and John Muir in nineteenth-century America.

Arguably the first, and certainly an eloquent and robust, eco-misanthrope was the Californian poet, Robinson Jeffers.

Describing himself as an "inhumanist", Jeffers was already alert in the 1930s to the environmental consequences of the "disastrous rhythm of dream-led masses" as they danced, "fractious and smug", to an alluring siren song of abundance, comfort and liberty.[18] We'll encounter Jeffers and his eco-misanthropic successors again in the following chapter.

IN DENIAL

The purpose of this lightning historical sketch of pessimism and misanthropy is not to convert readers to these positions. It serves, however, to scotch the idea that these dark visions are confined to a few German thinkers suffering from *Welt-schmerz* and some French existentialists depressed by the absurdity of human existence. Pessimism and misanthropy are perennial perspectives on the human condition, manifest in many philosophical and religious traditions. Once they are recognized as, essentially, judgements or assessments of our condition, and not just as moods or feelings, it is perverse to think they can be dismissed as pathological symptoms.

The very entrenchment of these judgements in traditions of philosophy and religion, both Eastern and Western, makes it all the more puzzling, however, why they are not more generally and popularly endorsed. Why is it that relatively few people acknowledge both the unhappiness and the related "moral disaster" of humankind? Why are so many people in denial about these?

The Buddha, we saw, made a start with addressing this question. The perception of suffering is uncomfortable, as also is admission of the extent of our vices and failings: hence there are understandable motives to remain ignorant of our actual condition. Indeed, several failings, such as vanity and self-pity, conveniently blind people to this condition. But in the modern world, there are several factors, both social and ideological, that also contribute to this blindness.

To begin with, there are the bright-siding, "booster-ish" messages by which people are now bombarded. School teachers, advertisers, vote-seeking politicians and congregation-seeking preachers all have an interest in con-vincing people, not only that their life can be good, but that *they* are good. Self-esteem has replaced humility as something to promote. "Everyone is beautiful/talented/a genius", "You can be whatever you want to be", "Everyone *deserves* to be happy", "Your opinion really matters to us", "You can make a difference!" – these are some of the slogans of our times. They seem to work. When people apologise for, say, a racist slur or misogynistic remark, they invariably say "This isn't what I am". The idea is that the real I, deep down, is good, despite my doing things which aren't. Religious teachers no longer refer to sin and the need for redemption: instead they speak of the "infinite value" each of us has in God's dispensation.

Then there is also the success, in richer countries, of keep-ing suffering out of sight. The Buddha, legend has it, was protected by his father from encountering old, diseased and dying people. It was when he did eventually meet with these "three divine messengers" of suffering that he embarked on his search for enlightenment. Today, hospices, nursing homes, windowless abattoirs and muzak-filled crematoriums protect us from the daily encounters of our not-so-distant ancestors with decay, pain and death.

Next is the tendency – encouraged by the media – to scapegoat. This is certainly salient in the case of environmen-tal depredation. Instead of an honest recognition that this is the inevitable penalty paid for a way of life in which we all participate – for a consumerist, "achievement" society – blame is directed, especially by so-called "eco-socialists", towards a familiar cast of villains. Free-market capitalists, multinational companies, "blah-blahing" political leaders, the far right... the list goes on.

The tendency to scapegoat flows from the optimistic illusion that it is not the human condition as such that is awful, but only certain conditions under which human beings live. Certainly, there is no need to deny that certain conditions – civil war, for example – do exacerbate types of suffering and favour particular moral failings, such as cruelty or brutality. But for the Buddha and other figures encountered in this chapter, it is shallow and deluded to fix the blame on, and confine a pessimistic verdict to, these especially adverse conditions. For these conditions are themselves only made possible by entrenched failings and vices of humankind. It is superficial, for instance, on the part of contemporary socialist commentators to suppose that destructive greed is confined to, and even the product of, capitalist systems and neoliberal ideology. Greed for wealth, land, power and status has in the past been no less apparent in the behaviour of oppressive feudal lords, land-grabbing African tribes, and the elite cadres of communist regimes.

A further factor that obstructs clear recognition of the human condition, is the sheer busyness of the hyperactive form of life we have developed, with its consequent anxieties and mental exhaustion. For, this is plainly unconducive to prolonged attention to our condition. As one Christian Desert Father observed, "because of the turbulence of life, the one who lives in the midst of activity does not see his sins".[19] The Buddha and Zhuangzi made comparable remarks a few centuries earlier, and the point they all make has even greater purchase today. Just as several of our failings serve to blind us to our failings, so dogged dedication to achievement, material wealth and status – with all the frustrations it will encounter – occludes recognition of itself and its consequent ills.[20]

These familiar social developments are complemented by a variety of intellectual or ideological positions that counter or diminish negative perceptions of the human condition. One is the continuing decline of religious beliefs, particularly in the possibility of everlasting hell. The fear that they might be punished by eternal damnation gives to sins or moral failings a salience and seriousness that mundane threats of reprimand or prison do not.

Then there is a popular view, expressed by people who boast of being "down to earth" and "living in the real world", that echoes the cynicism of the maxims of the Duc de la Rochefoucauld and Bernard Mandeville's *The Fable of the Bees*. The idea is that many of our failings are not only to be expected, but are actually necessary for keeping the wheels of society and the economy running smoothly. For an "achievement" society to emerge and be maintained, for example, a lot of people need to be ruthlessly ambitious and envious of the success of others. The strange conclusion drawn by the cynics is that our alleged vices and failings, given their strategic roles, are therefore not really vices or failings at all. Strange, since others would reasonably conclude that it surely strengthens an indictment of a way of life if its vices and moral failings are necessary to its maintenance.

If moral cynicism still exerts an influence, so does the European Enlightenment confidence in humanity's progress. Despite the horrors of the twentieth century, this conviction remains resilient. While the emphasis is often on advances in science and medicine, several recent authors have also told optimistic narratives of moral progress. (Cioran, incidentally, thought that the sole area in which progress could be discerned was hygiene.) It is an irony of these narratives that, by dwelling on the terrible history of humankind with which, allegedly, the present contrasts, they are liable to reinforce the misanthropic perception.

Many, certainly, will find these optimistic narratives uncompelling. A distinguished British moral philosopher was asked, a few years back, how he could retain his confidence in progress in the face of such moral catastrophes as the 1994 Rwanda genocide, in which 600,000 people were killed. "But that was twenty years ago!" came the reply. I want to respond, first, that twenty years is a very short time in which to measure humanity's progress and, second, that these were hardly two decades of moral innocence. They witnessed murderous civil wars, man-made famines, the mushrooming of drug cartels, terrorist atrocities . . . the list goes on. It is worth noting, too, that the optimists typically gloss over the enormous and ever-growing suffering inflicted by human beings on animals, through industrial farming, experimentation, recreational hunting, habitat destruction, and much else.

Have I exaggerated contemporary reluctance to countenance the verdicts on our condition of pessimism and misanthropy? Possibly, for there is at least one recent development that has prompted some attention to these verdicts. I refer to the use, or abuse, of social media. Trolling, betrayal of trust by posting intimate photos, death threats, hate mail, online child pornography, fake news, hysterical rants . . . these can hardly fail to awaken people to the unpleasantness, and worse, of human beings when they are able to demonstrate their perverse desires, aggression and treachery with little prospect of sanctions. The loud calls for greater policing of social media are an admission that, without a real threat of punishment, human beings are all too liable to indulge their failings. Thomas Hobbes, for one, would say "I told you so".

The misanthrope does not have to be a jaundiced cynic to hold that, at least in modern forms of life, people will generally act well only when there are motives to do so. One of those motives is fear of reprisal, ostracization, or punishment. When such constraints are missing or ineffective, as they largely are in the case of social media, the vices and failings that suffuse these forms of life are on full display.

It has not been my aim in this chapter to convince readers of the wisdom of pessimism and misanthropy. A much longer book than this one would be required for that task. Such a book would, for example, defend this wisdom against the charge that it relies on a questionable concept of "human nature". How, the critic might ask, can we be sure that our failings are the product of natural selection alone, and that history and culture have played no part? My response would be that the issue of human nature is a red herring. Perhaps it is possible to imagine recognizably human societies of the distant past – very small and simple ones, say, located in a land of milk and honey and blessed with supremely wise leaders – that were largely free from suffering, failings and vices. But pessimism and misanthropy are not refuted by such possibilities. For one can remain confident that the sufferings, failings and vices witnessed in history are not the ephemeral products of passing political, social and economic arrangements. Instead, they are entrenched in all civilizations remotely like our own, including those to which the Buddha, Zhuangzi and others who reflected on the darkness of our condition belonged. Pessimism and misanthropy are directed towards human life as

17

it has actually become and is very likely to remain – towards, that is, the human condition as we know it.

What I have tried to do in the present chapter, however, is to provide a sympathetic description of one great teacher's articulation of the wisdom of pessimism and misanthropy, the Buddha's. I have also briefly indicated the antiquity and persistence of this wisdom in various philosophical and religious traditions. Finally, I have exposed, and in some cases tried to discredit, some of the factors in modern life that obstruct acceptance of misanthropic pessimism. I hope that readers will, even if they do not embrace it, at least remain open to this perspective, for the rest of the book addresses the question of how it might best be responded and accommodated to in one's life.

2

Amnesia and nihilism

JUDGEMENTS, MOODS AND EMOTIONS

The question that each of us should be asking may be posed in a variety of ways: "How should I accommodate the pessimistic and misanthropic perspective?", "How should I adjust, shape and conduct my life in the light of it?", "How should this perspective inform my life?", or "What tone or stamp to my life should it give?" Before we consider some answers to this question, it calls for some elaboration.

First, I want to emphasize again its first-person character. It is not the question of what would be the most beneficial way for "us" – human beings in general – to respond to the harsh assessment of the human condition. Perhaps it would be good for people, animals and the planet if we travelled by aeroplane much less, but that does not settle whether I should take fewer flights. My situation might, in certain ways, be special or relevantly different from that of others, and anyway I am certain that most people are not going to give up flying. That various scenarios might be desirable is neither here nor there, as far as my decisions are concerned, unless they are also realistic. A focus on the merits or otherwise of unrealistic scenarios is an evasion of the question of how I should accommodate to pessimism and misanthropy.

Second, why does the question matter? Why should I want or need to make this accommodation? After all, I agree with any number of judgements about humankind – how it evolved, for instance, or its technological progress – but I don't usually ask how these should inform or shape my life. Or, rather, I won't ask this unless the judgement is one that challenges some settled conviction of mine. Darwin's account of human evolution did challenge certain Christian beliefs and many Christians indeed felt a need to accommodate this new theory of our origins. Likewise, the dark visions of the human condition expressed by powerful, persuasive voices like the Buddha's or Schopenhauer's can come as a shock to people who encounter them for the first time. By puncturing people's confidence in sunnier estimates of our condition, these dark perspectives are disturbing and disquieting, and call for a response.

It is important to stress, too, that the negative verdict on humankind is not a "mere" judgement, a matter of putting a tick against the statement "Humankind is awful!" – and then moving on. This might be the attitude of an undergraduate philosophy student writing an essay on some pessimistic aphorism of Schopenhauer's, but it is not the serious embrace of a position that expressions like "pessimistic perspective" or "misanthropic vision" are intended to convey.

Such a perspective or vision is serious in the double sense of being significant and sombre. The mood of someone who has internalized the perspective is not easy to shake off and is, at the least, uncomfortable and disquieting – a mood to be confronted, not shrugged off. Several of the figures encountered in the previous chapter express strong emotional reactions

20

to their perceptions of the human condition. Leopardi veers between "pity and derision" for humankind, Cioran expresses "disgust" for it, Swift "hatred" of it, and others speak of their "anguish" or "contempt". But none of these particular emotions are universal among pessimists and misanthropes, and they are best regarded as modulations of a more general mood.

"Mood", here, corresponds to the German word *"Stimmung"*, which can be translated as "mood", but also as "tuning" or "attunement". Unlike an emotion – a type of feeling – a mood is an attunement to the world, an affectively charged way in which it figures for, or presents itself to, someone. Moods hover between feelings and perceptions. Happiness and depression, for example, are not just "inner" states, but ways in which things, places and people appear and are experienced. "The world of the happy man is a different one from that of the unhappy man", remarked Ludwig Wittgenstein – "waxing" rather than "waning".[1]

For the mood appropriate to the dark perspective on the human condition, I'll use a relatively bland term I've already used a couple of times – "disquiet". No term is perfect, but this one captures something of the combination of unease and unhappiness that is surely the minimum that this perspective, if serious, engenders. Whether disquiet then modulates into, say, anguish, despair, pity or hate will depend on the circumstances and the temperament of the individual.

Whatever else disquiet is, it is unwelcome and unpleasant. It is something that, if it cannot or should not be expelled, needs to be accommodated or managed, taken up in a rational way that may even serve to enhance one's life. Disquiet is too disturbing to be simply ignored or waved away: that is why, if you endorse the pessimistic, misanthropic perspective, you are bound to ask how it can be accommodated.

21

So, I now turn to ways of responding to that perspective and its associated mood. They are the responses of people that I'll label amnesiacs, nihilists, activists and quietists respectively.

AMNESIA

A natural enough response to uncomfortable beliefs is to try to be rid of them – by refuting them, say, or simply setting them aside. The people I'm labelling "amnesiacs" are ones that psychologists call "motivated" or "repressive" amnesiacs – people who intentionally set aside and try to forget disquieting beliefs, attitudes and perspectives. The amnesiac does not so much accommodate pessimism and misanthropy as put them out of mind.

Amnesia comes in a variety of forms. One form is that of hedonism, though this too can take various shapes. What hedonistic amnesiacs share is the attempt to blot out a dark vision of the human condition through indulgence in pleasures. What may begin as a defiant refusal, in a *carpe diem* spirit, to become depressed by a bleak account of humankind ends with this account being forgotten or suppressed. One thinks, for example, of the "jazz age" figures in Scott Fitzgerald's novels, too devoted to a constant round of parties, sexual liaisons and soporific days in the sun to recall the disquiet that impelled them to this lifestyle in the first place. Other hedonists are of a less sybaritic kind – for example, nineteenth-century devotees of aestheticism, such as Théophile Gautier and Walter Pater, in search of the refined, "delicious sensations" that it was the purpose of life to enjoy.

22

Amnesia can be sought, very differently, by the work-aholic. Here, pessimism is driven out, not by sexual, aesthetic or gastronomic indulgence, but by relentless attention to tasks and duties. Reflection on the state of humankind gets dismissed as an annoying interruption in a demanding work schedule. Or, of course, amnesia may also be sought through alcohol, other intoxicants or narcotics. People often drink, the saying goes, to forget – and what they drink to forget could be the human condition as much as a failed love affair or financial ruin. Literature, certainly, is full of such figures – the consul in Malcolm Lowry's *Under the Volcano*, say, or characters in stories by Carson McCullers and John Cheever. Why, given the dangers, human beings continue to use intoxicants and narcotics is something many anthropologists find puzzling. Their role in helping to put the human condition out of mind, so as to get on with the business of life, may be part of an explanation.

I could go on, and readers will be able to provide other examples of how people induce forgetfulness of what their species is like. It would be shallow abruptly to dismiss motivated amnesia with pious accusations of selfishness and failure to face up to one's responsibilities. It is not unreasonable to try to become happier, to quell disquiet, and to banish incipient feelings of hatred towards humankind. Nevertheless, there are good reasons for rejecting amnesia as a strategy for managing pessimistic and misanthropic disquiet.

For a start, it is a fragile strategy, one all too likely to fail and then invite back in the very disquiet that it aimed to dis-pel. As the Buddha, Epicurus, Leopardi, Schopenhauer and many others have taught, the hedonistic pursuit of pleasures is liable to produce an oscillation between unsatisfied desires and bored or jaded satiety. The febrile work into which a per-son plunges to dull their disquiet might, one morning, strike them as pointless and worthless. And there is no need to list the familiar dangers of drink and drugs, including remorse and the return, now augmented, of depression at the human condition.

Second, the amnesiac strategies are liable to be replete, not only with types of suffering identified by the pessimist – unsatisfied cravings and anxiety, for example – but with several of the vices or failings listed by the misanthrope. Undisciplined desire is itself a failing, inconsistent with the shaping of a good life. Moreover, it breeds jealousy of those more successful in achieving what they want, as well as prejudiced perceptions both of one's situation and that of other people. The same could be said of the workaholic, envious of a high-flying colleague, and unable to appreciate the value of things outside the sphere of their work. It is unnecessary to list the failings that often characterize the lives of people who seek forgetfulness through drink or drugs, with the terrible consequences for themselves and others that these often cause.

In the context of this book's aims, however, a final reason for rejecting the amnesiac strategy is more pertinent. In a good sense, it is not really a response to pessimism and misanthropy at all. Recall the walker in my Prologue. He strove, certainly, to suppress – forget, if you like – feelings of hatred or anger that sometimes assailed him. But there was something "more abiding" that he did not want to shake off: his considered negative judgement on humankind's moral and spiritual condition. Now, amnesiacs, to the degree that they succeed, no longer make this judgement: the pessimistic, misanthropic vision, and disquieting mood, have been submerged in a life of concentrated pleasure, unremitting work or whatever. The amnesiac's life is no longer disturbed at all by this vision and mood. There can be no talk, therefore, of it "informing" that life, or being "managed" or "accommodated". It is a life of motivated ignorance, a life that is not led in the light of truth.

This is not – not yet, at least – to dismiss motivated amnesia. Perhaps, if all attempts genuinely to respond to, rather than suppress, the negative judgement fail, amnesia would remain *faute de mieux*. People would be advised to ignore St Benedict's command, "Flee forgetfulness!", or Kierkegaard's injunction to live "in the truth".[2] So, let's look at these attempts, beginning with what I label "nihilism".

NIHILISM

Immanuel Kant, whose several very negative observations on the moral texture of human life are often overlooked, distinguished several kinds of misanthrope. One of these he labelled "the Enemy of Mankind". The stance of this Enemy is "enmity", which combines "dislike", even hatred, of humankind, with "ill-will" towards it. The Enemy's aim is "to destroy the welfare of others".[3]

This is a good characterization of some of those I'm labelling "nihilists". Like amnesiacs, these people are not really concerned to accommodate misanthropy. Instead, they amplify it through splenetic tirades against humankind, thereby converting disquiet into hatred and a celebration of the disappearance of human beings.

But nihilism, again like amnesia, is a broad church, and not all nihilists are intemperate enemies of mankind. Many convey their misanthropy in cooler, more measured terms. What nihilists share, however, is a welcoming of the extinction of humankind, or at least a very large percentage of it. Many of them, moreover, not only welcome this prospect but work towards it, if only by advocacy through their writings and teachings. For example, Eduard von Hartmann, as we saw, hoped that his own books would eventually inspire human beings to collective suicide. It is unsurprising that advocacy is the main nihilist strategy, since other methods of extinguishing humankind are likely to run foul of the law. But, as we'll see, there are exceptions.

The rationale for nihilism is not hard to find. Impressed, like the Buddha, by the scale of suffering in the world – human and non-human – and by the human vices and failings largely responsible for this suffering, the nihilist concludes, like Sophocles' Chorus, that the ideal is for human beings not to exist. And in lieu of total annihilation, the fewer people there are the better. The way to be free of the disquiet caused by humankind's failings is by removing the source.

Splenetic nihilist rhetoric is especially marked among eco-misanthropes. If, the rhetoric seems to imply, human beings were only damaging themselves, that might be something to put up with. But, of course, they are also destroying natural environments and causing immense suffering for billions of animals. The only way to save these innocent victims is through the demise of humankind. Hence we find the architect and environmentalist, Ian McHarg, describing humankind as "a planetary disease", a species whose annihilation he "would not feel badly" about, given its treatment of "birds and bees" and innumerable other species.[4] A more recent eco-misanthrope declares herself "deeply saddened that there has never managed to be an annihilation of the human species", for this would be a "life-affirming event that could liberate the natural world from oppression".[5] In a similar vein, some nihilists welcomed the Covid-19 outbreak. Alleged to be the result of human interference in nature, not only did it contribute to reducing the population, but was an encouraging portent of more lethal pandemics to come.

Other eco-misanthropic nihilists do not join in cheering and celebrating the annihilation of humankind, even though they judge this to be good on balance. For an anti-natalist thinker, like Benatar, radical population reduction will substantially reduce the sum total of suffering by humans and animals alike. Then there are the so-called "transhumanist" thinkers whose goal is not the extinction of human beings but their conversion into beings of a different and higher kind – more intelligent, more virtuous, more artistic, and so on. Here is an exception to the nihilists' general strategy of working towards their goal only through advocacy and teaching. For there are currently scientists at work on developing the robots, computers, and AI systems that, they believe, will eventually embody minds vastly superior to the human ones they will replace. It is not, then, the extinction of humankind *tout court* that the future holds in store, but its apotheosis – its transformation into a higher form of existence no longer, as Nietzsche put it, "botched and bungled" like our own.

Nihilism should not, with its understandable rationale, be lightly dismissed. It must be taken seriously, for example, by those Buddhists who accept the doctrine of rebirth. The promise of the Buddha is that eventually – after countless aeons and innumerable rebirths – all sentient beings will achieve nirvana, a term that means "to become extinguished" in the sense that the flame of a candle gets extinguished. Here is not the place to inquire if this is extinction *simpliciter* or only of conscious life in any remotely familiar form. Whatever it is, extinction is the only way to guarantee an end to the massive preponderance of suffering over happiness, and therefore one that good Buddhists must advocate.

27

The Buddha, however, would not have joined in any raucous celebration of the death of humankind. The extinction of humankind, even if it would be a good thing, no more calls for celebration than does a deer cull or the execution of drug traffickers, beneficial as it might be. It is clear that this brand of nihilism, like motivated amnesia, exhibits several of the vices and failings that drew misanthropic criticism in the first place. The remarks quoted earlier from enthusiasts for splenetic nihilism display, at a minimum, hatred, absence of compassion, and emotional excess.

Nihilism, however, even of a cooler, more moderate kind, cannot be the best response to pessimism, misanthropy and disquiet. This is because it cannot provide the person seeking to accommodate these with any guidance. The Buddha – though not, unfortunately, plenty of later Buddhists – recognized this. The primary goal for each person must be his or her liberation from suffering and human evil, not the unimaginably distant one of universal extinction.

There are two reasons why nihilism provides no guidance or accommodation. First, the scenario of the foreseeable annihilation, total or near total, of humankind is too much of a fantasy to inform and influence my life. The same is true of the transhumanist scenario of our morphing into a superior form of intelligent beings. One cannot, of course, completely exclude the possibility of a meteorite, a virus, or a nuclear conflict that will put an end to human life – or of a take-over by super-robots who then replace us. Plenty of novels and films depict such possibilities. But only novelists, filmmakers, eccentrics or academics who enjoy, or profit from, speculating on these matters could let their lives be shaped by such scenarios.

Consider, for example, the anti-natalist proposal. The fact

is, as Benatar recognizes, that no more than a small fraction of the population will decide not to have children. Even if I agreed, therefore, that it would be a good thing if no one were to have children – since it will put an end to humankind – this implies nothing about how I should act. It does not even imply that I should have no children. To suppose it does is like thinking that approval of the communist fantasy of a world without individual ownership implies that I should now give away my house and car. Sophocles' anti-natalist injunction is best seen, perhaps, not as the conclusion of his pessimism and misanthropy, but as an especially stark and dramatic way of giving force to these judgements.

But suppose I'm wrong about the nihilist scenarios being fantasies. Suppose that, in the foreseeable future, a serious movement towards radical population reduction, or towards the replacement of human beings by robots, gathered momentum. Suppose that anti-humanist, transhumanist, or anti-natalist proposals were no longer simply topics of amusing chatter, academic journal articles, or sensationalist tabloid headlines. Would nihilism then help me to make a practical accommodation with my pessimism and misanthropy?

The question prompts the second reason why nihilism can provide no guidance for me. Unless I am one of a very tiny number of people, my contribution to the nihilist cause is going to be negligible. (This tiny number might include people with a finger on a nuclear button and Bond-like villains with the power and wealth to develop and spread devastatingly lethal viruses.) My contribution – donating to futuristic research in robotics, say, or trying to convert lecture audiences to anti-natalism – will be vanishingly small. This might not matter if I didn't have other things to do with my time and energy, but I do, including other and perhaps more

29

effective ways of responding to misanthropic disquiet. I might, for example, decide that donating for the relief of the suffering of certain people or animals is a better and more effective contribution than supporting robotics research.

A possible reply to the points I've just made is that there can be reasons for supporting some cause even when one knows that it is an unrealistic one or that one's own contribution to its furtherance is indiscernibly small. Perhaps it is "noble" to fight for hopeless causes, or a duty incumbent on me to support a cause irrespective of the effectiveness of my participation. The place to consider this reply is in the following chapters, on activism and quietism, for the point recurs in the context of discussing better subscribed responses than nihilism to the negative verdict on humankind.

Nihilism is a tendency that is bound, in certain moods, to seem attractive to pessimists and misanthropes. Let's agree, however, that the unrealistic nature of its goals and the inability of ordinary individuals to help realize these goals, even if they were less improbable, are good reasons to consider other forms of response to the negative verdict.

3

Activism

MELIORISM AND "CONCERTED EFFORT"

For amnesiacs, the way to be rid of disquiet is to blot the condition of humankind out of one's thoughts; for the nihilist the way is to be rid of humankind, the source of the disquiet. Both strategies give up too soon, according to the champions of the response to pessimism and misanthropy that I shall consider in this chapter. According to them, disquiet is to be overcome, or at least managed, not by forgetting or bringing to an end the human condition, but by working towards its betterment. We should not ignore, but on the contrary be alert to this condition and, instead of despairing at it, undertake to improve it.

This activist, meliorist response is the most common one found among people who are nevertheless receptive to a dark vision of the human condition. Among them are those who march, demonstrate, protest and otherwise visibly display their support for movements dedicated to ways that, they believe, will lead to the melioration of humankind. These people include, among many others, radical environmentalists, anti-racists, pacifists, religious evangelists, nationalistic populists, and enforcers of "woke" cultural policies.

It might be thought that activism and meliorism are ruled out by pessimism. But pessimism comprises two judgements: a recognition that the human condition is a bad one, in which suffering predominates, and a prediction that this situation will not radically alter. People who confine themselves to the first judgement may well hope that suffering and moral failings can be significantly reduced through movements like those mentioned. There is no inconsistency in the title of a recent blog entitled "The world is awful ... The world can be much better". But these are not the words, of course, of someone who accepts the full pessimist package.

It is, moreover, theoretically possible to accept the whole pessimist package and still advocate activist intervention for the betterment of humankind. This is because a negative prospect of future improvement can come in different degrees of gloom. Rousseau, for instance, thought it was possible to "banish" some – but only some – vices. William James thought there was a reasonable, though not guaranteed, prospect of betterment, and hence described himself as standing between optimism and pessimism. With greater, but not total, pessimism Aldo Leopold, the pioneering ecologist and proponent of "the land ethic", stated that implementation of this ethic "would appear hopeless, but for the minority which is in obvious revolt" against, for example, the mechanization of farming.[1] Provided people think that the prospect of radical betterment is not completely negligible, they can be both pessimists, as defined, and committed to working for its realization.

It's worth noting, in passing, that it is possible to believe in the betterment of humankind without thinking that activist commitment is required. Perhaps a god will descend and usher in a new dawn for humankind. Or, maybe the betterment will come about naturally, as several European Enlightenment thinkers supposed. In their optimistic vision, improved education, better living standards, greater commerce, and the decline of religious superstition would all contribute to "the perfection of mankind", without any need for revolutions, demonstrations, and muscular allegiance to "causes".[2]

For those less sanguine than these eighteenth-century figures, however, the path to perfection is not smooth: indeed, it requires massive dedication and action if it is to be cleared. Meliorism, that is, requires activism. "Activists", as I intend the term, does not refer simply to people who are active in ways that, they hope, will make situations better and reduce suffering. A very large number of us might be like that. Rather, I have in mind something like the media do when they refer to activists, showing images of, say, people gluing themselves to a motorway or otherwise demonstrating in protest against oil, war, capitalism, abortion or whatever.

The activist credo is that the human condition can be radically improved through concerted, committed, collective effort. The activist eco-misanthrope, for example, thinks that, through such effort, the planet can be "saved" and that the exploitation and devastation of the earth can be brought to a halt by the bold and perhaps aggressive interventions of dedicated cadres of engaged environmentalists.

The aims of activism are "big", "global" even – world peace, salvation of the planet, race and gender equality, "true" democracy, and so on. And, of course, they need to be big if achievement of the aims is seriously to be described as bettering the human condition, reducing the scale of human suffering, or correcting human failings. The activist, in the proposed sense, is not content with bringing about small-scale, local benefits – helping old and infirm people to get around, say, or volunteering at a shelter for abandoned pets. Indeed, activists can be scornful of such modest enterprises – like the eco-activist on a radio programme who derided people for focusing on the protection of a local river rather than the whole biosphere. The ambitious activist ideal is the elimination of what a character in an Aldous Huxley novel calls all the "unnecessary, home-made sorrows" of the world.[3]

REMINDERS

How should activism be judged as a response or accommodation to the pessimistic, misanthropic view of humankind? This, some will say, is too broad a question, for there are – as the examples above indicate – many activist causes, some of which are more attractive than others. But I suggest that, quite generally, activist commitment is not a compelling strategy for coping with disquiet at the human condition.

Before that, however, it is useful to remind ourselves of certain matters that are too easily ignored. Doing so will help to dispel the air of *obviousness* that the good of activism now has for many, especially young, people – to highlight, in effect, their moral myopia. First, we should remember that the activist ideal is a recent historical development. In older cultures, East and West, the idea that people should devote their lives to supporting large-scale social and political causes was, when considered at all, criticized and rejected. In the traditions of these cultures, including Buddhism, Daoism, Epicureanism and Christianity, the paramount concern of a person should be with care of the self or soul. That this should be ignored in favour of dedication to remote global goals would have been judged a form of both delusion and moral evasion. This was true even for those thinkers, like Aristotle, who commended participation in political life. The goal of participation was not the betterment of humankind, but the good of the *polis*, engagement with which was one of the virtues that made for a flourishing individual life.

Second, we should recall the terrible record of many activist programmes, including those inspired by communist and militant religious ideologies. The brutal pursuits of seemingly noble causes – an end to alienated labour, a retrieval of true religiosity – have resulted in great moral crimes and immeasurable suffering. To judge from some eco-misanthropic rhetoric – with its calls for human "die-backs" and absolute equality of wealth – comparably brutal methods are still being proposed for the achievement of activist goals.

Someone will reply that other activist causes in history, including the recent past, have not had terrible outcomes, and have brought about greater justice. Sadly, it is easier to discern the very visible suffering caused by, say, Soviet and Maoist socio-economic experiments, than to judge the effect on well-being of successful struggles for justice and rights. These struggles are only threads in the great complex of a civilization that has been productive of immense suffering – through warfare, industrialization, destructive technologies, warped ideologies, the frenetic pursuit of material wealth, the collapse of protective family structures, and much else that bring in their wake loss, loneliness, fear and anxiety. It is difficult to the point, perhaps, of impossibility to isolate and reckon the impact of this or that activist cause on a society's well-being, let alone that of the wider world. Even in cases where it may be possible to identify large-scale reduction in suffering and an overall enhancement of well-being, the contribution of activism remains hard to judge. Improvement may owe much more to advances in technology, nutrition and medicine, for example.[4] As George Eliot observed, we should allow that often enough "the growing good of the world is partly dependent on unhistoric acts", not grand or heroic interventions.[5] There is a tendency to magnify the contribution of reformers and revolutionaries, at the expense of, say, pharmacologists and hygienists. (Although, caution is required here, too: one would need to balance, for instance, the benefits of life-prolonging drugs against the travails of old age.)

If the meliorist impact of activist fights for justice is uncertain, then a third reminder is also apposite. In nearly all earlier cultures, moral concern for "strangers", as well as for family and friends, was primarily one for their well-being, and not for protecting their human rights. The notion of such rights and their violation does not figure, even implicitly, in the teachings of the Buddha, Socrates, Confucius and Jesus. This reminder should make us ask whether prioritization of rights, equality and justice is a contemporary predilection rather than the enactment of an obvious moral truth that we enlightened moderns have discovered. Certainly, as we have just seen, it should not be assumed that establishing rights and equality is any guarantee of well-being and reduction in suffering.

FAILINGS

There is even less reason to think that social and political activism has achieved any mitigation of the vices and failings that, for the misanthrope, invite a negative moral verdict on humankind. On the contrary, activism provides scope and encouragement for several of these failings.

It is instructive, here, to recall some ancient teachings

in which this point is anticipated. The Buddha, Zhuangzi, Epicurus and Augustine were not confronted with anything like today's political activism, but it is not difficult to infer from their remarks on kingship and politics what their response to it would be. It is sometimes said that neither were they confronted by the kinds of issues – global warming, say – which inspire contemporary activism. If they had been around today, the suggestion goes, they might well have supported activist causes. I see no reason at all to suppose this is true: the reasons these ancient thinkers give for rejecting activism apply as much today as to their own times. That their times were very different from ours does nothing to impugn those reasons and the conceptions of the good life from which they are drawn.

None of these figures was an anarchist, but each of them held that, in present-day parlance, the state should be a "minimal" one. The job of the ruler is to protect people and their property from violence and damage, and to ensure, as the Buddha emphasizes, that the "needy" are looked after. (This was not, incidentally, on egalitarian grounds, but because poverty leads to crime and so to social breakdown.)[6] For the author of the *Daodejing*, the sage ruler does as little as possible, treating his state like a small fish that should be cooked lightly and without fuss, lest it break apart.[7]

Crucially, these teachers agree that wise persons should have as little truck with politics and government as possible. The wise are "free from the prison of politics", declared Epicurus. Zhuangzi rejected an offer of high office: better, he said, to live naturally, like a turtle wallowing in mud, than to work in a temple or palace. Augustine wrote that the person engaged in the public, political realm is "a traveller in a foreign land". The Buddha's main discourse on kingship is set in the context of advice to his monks to "keep to your own preserves", to be "islands unto yourselves".[8]

As these remarks suggest, several reasons are at work in this suspicion of political involvement. It compromises one's freedom; it is an artificial way of living; it distracts from both higher concerns and pressing local issues, and so on. But at work, too, is appreciation of the vices and failings of political life. Rivalry, anger, self-righteousness, hatred, delusion, "lust for domination", as Augustine called it[9] – these and many more are encouraged by political engagement and exploited by the leaders of activist movements. Which observers of political movements, especially those driven by ideologies, would want to deny the accuracy of these accusations?

They are accusations, moreover, that easily convert into suspicion of social and political activism. It is hard, for example, not to be struck by the fury, hate, and self-righteousness that distort the faces of many of today's protesters as they rail against those who have attracted their wrath. Many of them fit the description by a Buddhist character in Aldous Huxley's novel, *Island*, of people who "always feel impelled to Do Something, and are never inhibited by doubts, qualms, by sympathy or sensibility".[10]

Other accusations can be added. The tendency, for example, of protests, disingenuously advertised as "peaceful", to turn, predictably, into violence. Or, the degree of "virtue signalling" that is apparent among many activists: a desire to parade their moral credentials, irrespective of the chances of their cause succeeding. Or the lazy mindlessness that makes so much activism look like a war against whoever is reluctant to endorse some simplistic slogan.

The judgement on activism of the thinkers I just cited would be an extension of their criticism of participation in politics. It is a mark of wise rule, according to the *Daodejing*, that people do not become "contentious", and instead of shouting about "righteousness" and the good of humanity, live quietly and simply, concerned more with the welfare of their families than with "causes".[11] When the Buddha describes how people should live when society has recovered from the violence caused by neglect of the "needy", nothing remotely like social and political engagement is mentioned.[12] Instead, he exhorts them to refrain from envy, sexual misconduct and greed, and to respect their parents and the heads of their clan.

Implicit in the case against activism is condemnation of the frenetic busyness – the relentless focus on goals and achievements – that demonstrations and protests so saliently manifest. Not only is it fuelled by some of our worst failings, such as the desires for domination and fame, but it gives rise to the anxieties and disappointments that are destructive of happiness and tranquillity. For Epicurus, this destruction is the reason why he was "disgusted" by politics. For the Buddha, activists are among those who, ignoring the injunction to "keep to your own preserves", spend their time "hankering and fretting for the world". And Augustine would surely include them among those people whose ambitions and goals, "wishes and lusts . . . hurry and drag them hither and thither", and deeper into that "foreign land" that is not humankind's proper abode.[13]

There's a further vice or failing highlighted in much ancient literature. This is hubris – a cocktail of arrogance, overconfidence and a conviction of superiority – to which human beings, both individually and collectively, are prone. One thinks of the Greek myths, like that of Prometheus, which caution against it, or the Buddha's inclusion of "conceit" or "pride" (*māna*) among the "fetters" that bind people to the cycle of rebirth. Hubris is especially evident today in environmental activism. There is some irony here, since hubris is, not unreasonably, blamed by activists for the dominion over nature that has brought with it environmental devastation. But in several respects, hubris typically infects their own causes.

First, as one disillusioned environmentalist observes, activism encourages in people an exaggerated sense of "self-importance" – of, for example, their special role in "saving the planet" or "engineering some grand shift in consciousness".[14] Second, activism often betrays misplaced confidence in human capacities. Belief, for example, in the power of technology and democratic politics to prevent further environmental degradation. Or, faith in a basic niceness of people that will help them to welcome the radical changes in lifestyles that serious, indeed Draconian, policies to combat further degradation will entail.

Third, despite the rhetoric of "saving the earth" and preventing "the end of nature", it is clear that the recent explosion of support for environmental causes is due to fear that the well-being specifically of human beings, including the activists themselves, is severely threatened by climate change. For the novelist and essayist, Jonathan Franzen, preoccupation with global warming shows that many people "only care about the planet if they personally are threatened".[15] Certainly, the youthful supporters of movements like Extinction Rebellion seem partly motivated by the prospect of their generation suffering the economic consequences of their elders' irresponsible treatment of the natural world.

Today's environmental activists look, then, to be as guilty of hubris as those against whom they fulminate. Human beings, it seems, have the right to determine how the natural

world shall be in accordance with what is perceived to benefit them. Turning moorland into wind farms, deserts into
acres of sun-reflectors, lochs into salmon farms, and many
other forms of the destruction of wild places are justified in
the name of sustaining an acceptable and comfortable level of
human life. For what is threatened is not "nature" – which will
of course survive, with its myriad forms of life – but a human
lifestyle. And the assumption of a human prerogative to shape
the natural world in order to preserve this lifestyle precisely
illustrates what the Greeks meant by hubris.

Hubris, of course, is not confined to environmental activism. One thinks, for example, of the way in which people in
Western liberal societies who parade their commitment to
sexual rights and freedoms are airily dismissive of other cultures, often religious ones, where these are not found. They
are perceived as primitive or child-like cultures whose citi-
zens are incapable of recognizing the self-evident truths of
liberal morality. Here, hubris merges with the dogmatism and
self-righteousness that are among the other failings to which
activism is prone.

REALISM

The final concerns I raise about activism as a response to pessimism, misanthropy and the disquiet they cause recall points
made about the nihilist response in Chapter 2. These are concerns about a lack of realism of which activists are typically
guilty.

I noted, towards the end of the previous section, the hubris
of much environmental activism. This self-importance on the
part both of individuals and collectives is due, in part, to belief

in the achievability of what are, in truth, unrealistic goals. The belief that we have the ability to avert the massively disruptive effects of climate change is unreasonable, even more so when it consists of confidence in engineering a revolution in people's desires, ambitions and consciousness. The hope of many environmentalists that the Covid pandemic would reconcile people to a simpler, more pared down lifestyle was soon dashed. Demands for higher wages, air travel, rapid economic growth and so on, quickly revived. Part of the answer, one fears, to the question posed in the title of Franzen's essay *What If We Stopped Pretending?* (that environmental disaster can be averted) is that we won't stop – and, indeed, that we don't want to stop.

Lack of realism is not, of course, confined to environmental activism. Quite generally, ambitious aspirations, inspired by the idea of "the perfectibility of humankind", radically to reduce the scale of suffering and human failings, involve fantasy and delusion. The unhappiness, disquiet, fears and anxieties that characterize the human condition are, as pessimists recognize, not the passing product of social and political forces, but of structures and processes of desire and thought that have come to be entrenched in that condition. The same is true of the vices and failings exposed by the misanthrope. The wholesale transformation of human purposes, emotions and self-understanding that would be required to remedy the situation of humankind is quite beyond anything that even the most muscular activism might bring about.

Resistance to accepting this is due, in large part, to some of our failings, for these occlude, as we saw in Chapter 1, a clear-sighted vision of the human condition. Activist enthusiasm and faith are buoyed up by "boosterish" bright-siding of the effectiveness of activism, sustained by the hubris of utopian projects, given credence through the scapegoating of easy targets, and fuelled by an unthinking impulse to "Do Something".

None of the ancient thinkers cited earlier in this chapter, recall, held out the prospect of melioration of the human condition through social and political activism. For the Buddha, Zhuangzi, Epicurus and Augustine alike, a few people may, through practices of self-cultivation, become free from both suffering and failings. But this is a liberation enabled, not by activist engagement, but by retreat from the business of the everyday world of engagements. It is in a monastery or a sheltered garden that liberation or emancipation is more sensibly sought than in public squares given over to protest and demonstration.

That these ancient figures did hold out the prospect of liberation and happiness is sometimes taken as evidence of their optimism. But it is surely a funny kind of optimism that confines this prospect to a few people – sages, monks, a group of reclusive philosophers, or recipients of God's grace – possessing remarkable gifts. Indeed, it would be a deeply ironic optimism that reserved the prospect of true happiness to beings that have, in essence, transcended a human way of life. If pessimism is understood, as I have been understanding it, as a judgement on the human condition, it is not contradicted by the prospect of a happier state beyond, or transcendent of, this condition.

Exaggerated faith in the feasibility of their causes is not the only lack of realism that activists display. Activists are also guilty of an unrealistic estimate of their individual impact upon or contribution to the causes they support. This is not surprising, perhaps, given how they are constantly being told how much of a difference they can make. Here is a brief selection of titles or sub-titles from some recent manuals for prospective activists: "How to change the world in 5 minutes, 1 hour or a day", "A pocket guide to making a difference", "Why politics has gone wrong and how you can help fix it", "Do something: Activism for everyone", and "No one is too small to make a difference".

The messages conveyed here belong to a wider tendency in the contemporary world to boost and bolster people's sense of their importance and worth. They are akin to such exhortations as "You can become whatever you want to be!" or "Follow your *own* dream!". They are also entirely misleading. We saw, when discussing nihilism, that only a very small number of people – with exceptional power, influence or luck – could do anything effective to try to implement a nihilistic programme. A similar point applies to activism. Even if activist goals were more realistic than I suggested, the difference that you or I can make to their achievement is vanishingly small. Unless, that is, you or I happen, like the leader of a powerful nation or a global superstar, to be very exceptionally placed.

This kind of unrealism is recognized by several former, or "recovered", environmental activists. Moreover, they point out, it is not the illusion of "making a difference" that is by itself the problem, but also the way it diverts attention away from the modest things that people actually can do to enhance their environments and connect to the natural world. As Franzen, once more, puts it, the "false hope of salvation" that drives activists distracts from, say, the work one could do in restoring a local woodland. Or, as Paul Kingsnorth more romantically writes, once I "withdraw from the campaigning and the marching", and am rid of the "false assumptions" that inspired it, I can instead "go out walking . . . listen to the wind and see what it tells me".[16]

There is a general point that emerges here. Commitment to an activist cause, if it is to be at all responsible and authentic, demands time, energy and thought, including moral reflection. The question is whether all of this can be worth it if one's support for the cause does nothing to improve its chance of success. After all, I have work to do, other people to care about, interests to pursue: in short, I have a life to lead, one that I should try to make a good one. Can it really serve in making my life better to devote time, effort and hard critical reflection to goals whose achievement I can do next to nothing to bring about? It is obvious, I take it, that those activists – mere virtue signallers, say, or seekers after camaraderie – who are unwilling to devote any of this attention to their causes are not responsible supporters and, for that reason, should find something else to do with their time.

There will be some readers who think that lack of realism is not an objection to activism. (A similar thought about nihilism was mentioned at the end of Chapter 2.) Is there not a certain moral heroism and nobility in people pursuing goals that they know are unrealistic or ones to which their own contribution is vanishingly small? "That the situation is hopeless", Aldo Leopold once remarked, "should not prevent our doing our best".[17] Isn't he right? Not in my judgement. For one thing, the examples sometimes given to establish the value of hopeless activism are, on inspection, irrelevant. One author, for instance, admires the "determination" of a Black woman who continued to "resist" racial discrimination, despite recognizing it as "hopeless resistance".[18] The woman continued to resist, she explained, because she "lives to harass white folk". But, in that case, the goal she pursues is no longer the "hopeless" one of ending discrimination, but the perfectly feasible one of "harassing" white people. She's comparable to a communist who, abandoning all hope of the proletarian revolution, still finds plenty of ways to *épater les bourgeois*.

Secondly, the choice facing people who recognize either the hopelessness of a cause or their own negligible contribution to it is not a binary one between futile protest and doing nothing else with their lives. They could do something better and less self-defeating. If they don't, the suspicion must be that they are motivated, not by a burning sense of injustice or whatever, but by a desire to signal their moral credentials to their peers.

It would have been obvious to the ancient thinkers on whom I have been drawing that there are better ways to live – and to accommodate the pessimistic and misanthropic verdicts on the human condition – than devotion to causes that are not only unrealistic or beyond the power of nearly all individuals to further, but hospitable as well to human vices and failings. Among these thinkers, too, there was a consensus on at least the general form that management of the disquiet that accompanies these verdicts must take. I turn to this accommodation – quietism, as I'll call it – in the next chapter.

4

Quietism

So far, I have considered three strategies for coping with the disquiet occasioned by a pessimistic and misanthropic perception of humankind. None of them succeed as ways to accommodate this perception in one's life. Amnesia is, in effect, an evasion of it, while nihilism and activism, in addition to their lack of realism, give rein to many of the failings that invited a negative verdict on the human condition.

I now turn to another way – or set of ways – of responding to pessimism and misanthropy and managing the disquiet that accompanies them. I call it "quietism". In Chapter 5, we'll encounter a variety of quietist ways, or strategies, of living. Before that, however, we need to identify the aspirations that are common to quietists, whichever ways they then take to realize aims in their lives. We need to have an understanding of quietism sufficiently general to fit its several forms – a description of what it is to live in a quietist key.

We'll arrive at this understanding through looking at a number of traditions or approaches in politics, religion and philosophy that have been labelled "quietist". The quietism

47

that I'll be characterizing is not identical with any of these traditions, but it includes elements and aspirations found in all of them.

Let's begin with the label "political quietist", sometimes applied to people who eschew not only socio-political activism, but almost all involvement in political affairs. Typically, the label is applied pejoratively, by those critical of such political abstinence. For these critics, quietism is irresponsible and guilty of apathy and indifference. There is, for example, a lot of discussion in the Islamic world of political quietism. Inspired by such texts as "Obey those in authority among you" (Q 4.59), some thinkers, Sunnis and Shiites alike, have taught avoidance of political participation. In doing so, they have invited the "political quietist" label from their opponents, who accuse them of encouraging either apathy or blind obedience.[1]

I intend nothing pejorative when referring to quietists: on the contrary, I shall be arguing for certain modes of quietism. Whether the quietist is a political quietist in the above sense, he or she is certainly no political activist, and for the reasons given in Chapter 3 for the rejection of activism. Unlike the activist, the quietist accepts or is resigned to the human condition being what it is, and entertains no meliorist or utopian ambitions. Humility requires abandonment not only of such ambitions, but of illusions about one's own power to "make a difference" through joining "causes". Rid of these ambitions and illusions, a person will want to be, to a significant degree, detached or disengaged from a context that is an arena for activist political causes. Such a person might hope – like the former, "recovering" environmentalists mentioned in the previous chapter – to experience a tranquillity or equanimity unavailable to the activist.

Quietism, however, cannot consist solely of a rejection of activism. Recall some of the amnesiacs from Chapter 2, such as the hedonist and workaholic. Neither of these is likely to be an activist, but it would be peculiar to refer to someone in constant and frenetic pursuit of pleasure, or someone obsessively committed to work projects, as quietist in character or lifestyle. Activists are what quietists will *not* be, but we also need to know something about what they *will* be. Still, in describing the quietist's rejection of activism, certain aspirations – detachment, for instance – were indicated that will recur in religious and other tendencies that have attracted the label "quietist". These are aspirations to be included in the portrait of the quietist we are working our way towards.

RELIGION AND QUIETISM

Here is the principal meaning of "quietism" given in the Shorter Oxford English Dictionary: "Religious mysticism based on the teaching of the Spanish priest Miguel de Molinos (*c*.1640–1697), rejecting outward forms of devotion in favour of passive contemplation and extinction of the will." Quietism here refers to the Roman Catholic movement, inspired by Molinos, that briefly flourished, especially in France, at the end of the seventeenth century. Only briefly, since both Molinos and his admirer, Madame Guyon – a "great and beautiful soul", according to Schopenhauer[2] – were imprisoned for heresy.

This Christian quietism was, like meliorist activism, but of a diametrically opposite kind, a response to pessimism and misanthropy.[3] The recognition of humankind's "dreadful vices" and "depravity" ought, these quietists wrote, to spur the soul to "abandon itself unto God", and avoid entanglement in worldly affairs. The properly humble person will accept and be resigned to the way humankind is, without any vain ambition to "rectify the exterior" world.

It was from much more than rectifying the world, however, that the Molinists prescinded. Abandonment unto God meant disengaging from almost all intercourse with "outward things", including "good works" in the community and even Church rituals. The performance of virtuous actions must not detract from contemplation of God. Contemplation was understood as passive receptivity to God's word, and not as philosophical reasoning or intellectual "meditation". The truly humble contemplative must, moreover, detach the soul not just from outward things, but from such "tyrants" as the passions and the will. The devout will "die to corruptions" and "appetites". Indeed, each of them will, as it was put, "die to the self".

The reward for humility, submission and detachment is not just "the union of the soul with God" in which "Christian perfection" consists. It is also the "repose, tranquillity and peace" that, for example, Mary, experiences, once she is no longer, like her sister Martha, "worried and distracted" by worldly tasks (Luke 10.41-2), so that "the Spirit of Christ might act in her". As Archbishop Fénelon, a Molinist sympathizer, reminded his readers, a desire to find happiness in the form of tranquillity is a perfectly legitimate one.[4]

The label "quietism" may have been coined for the Molinist doctrines, but it soon acquired a more general use, so that it is now common to find it attached to related religious views or tendencies. We read, for example, of the quietism of the Desert Fathers during the third to fifth centuries. The story is told of three monks in search of holiness, two of whom set off to do good works – to resolve conflicts and to visit the sick, respectively – while the third becomes a hermit in the desert. The former are soon disillusioned, and visit the hermit, who explains to them that anyone who lives and acts "in a crowd", with all its turbulence, cannot "see his sins" and find God.[5]

The writings of medieval German mystics, like Meister Eckhart and Johannes Tauler, have also been described as quietist. Certainly, one finds in their writings many of the ingredients of seventeenth-century quietism: acceptance of the world and humankind as they are, submission to God, detachment from worldly affairs, self-abnegation, and humility concerning the powers of human understanding. The "spirit of busyness" is rejected in favour of the serene tranquillity (*Gelassenheit*) that comes with disengagement, control of the will, and surrender to God.[6]

The quietist label has not been confined to Christianity, being extended, for instance, to Sufi teachings on "dying to self" before one's actual death. It was extended, too, by analogy with Christian quietism, to Buddhist schools, especially some sects of the Pure Land Buddhism that continue to flourish in Japan. For the medieval founders of these sects, the condition of humankind is a parlous one, for they were living, they believed, in the last and "degenerate" era of the Buddhist cosmological cycle – that of "the end of dharma" (*mappō*). According to the most popular of the sects, human beings are quite incapable of exercising "self-power" in order to progress towards enlightenment, and must rely instead on the "other-power" of the Buddha Amida. Through unquestioning faith in his power, people will be admitted by him into his "pure land", where enlightenment may be achieved. The proper manifestation of this faith is not moral practice, deeds, asceticism or meditative effort, but constant and grateful invocation of Amida's name. Confident of this Buddha's grace, people experience serenity and equanimity in anticipation of an end to suffering.

PHILOSOPHICAL QUIETISM

If the term quietism is now common in literature on religion, the expression "philosophical quietism" has also become familiar. It can, however, be taken in different ways – as the name of an approach to philosophical questions, as a philosophical account of the good life, and as a claim about the role of philosophy within that life. I'll consider these in turn.

As the name of an approach to philosophical enquiry, quietism was coined in the 1990s with reference to a view ascribed to Ludwig Wittgenstein. "Philosophy", he had written in his first book, "is not a body of doctrine but an activity ... [that] consists essentially in elucidations".[7] Later, he was to write that philosophy "leaves everything as it is", telling us nothing about the world that we don't already know. The philosopher's only legitimate task is to put an end to the compulsion to ask substantive, metaphysical questions about the world. This task is, in effect, like "the treatment of an illness", and when the treatment is successful, it "gives philosophy peace". It is this mention of peace, of course, that prompted the quietist label.[8]

Just as with the use of quietist within religion, so within philosophy the label was then applied more widely – to any thinker who rejected the enterprise of addressing and answering substantive questions about how the world or reality fundamentally is. It has been applied, for example, to the Buddha, Zhuangzi, Pyrrhonian sceptics, Montaigne, and various pragmatists and postmodernists. All of them, it is said, advocate disengagement from traditional philosophical questioning that seeks answers from theories of reality.

The reasons given for this disengagement vary considerably. It may be – as some of Wittgenstein's remarks indicate – that questions like "How do I know that other people feel pain?" are, on inspection, senseless, a sort of unobvious nonsense that needs to be exposed. Or it may be, as the Greek Sceptics held, that truth is simply inaccessible, since the arguments pro and con any belief cancel each other out. Or, as in the Daoist classics, it may be that knowledge of what matters – the Way (*dao*) – is an inarticulable, ineffable "know how", not an intellectual or theoretical kind of understanding. Or perhaps it is simply that, as the Buddha held, it is fruitless or "unprofitable" to pursue questions about eternity, the relation between soul and body, and the like. These have no bearing on the one issue that, according to him, really matters – suffering and its overcoming. As a robust empiricist, he may also have thought that the questions were senseless, since they could not be settled by experience.

The thinkers we've mentioned have more in common than simply recommending disengagement from metaphysical issues. They all, for a start, recommend acceptance of or submission to certain things – things that we should neither challenge nor try to justify. Wittgenstein, for example, held that there are "hinge propositions" – like "the world didn't begin five minutes ago" – that are presupposed by all our enquiries, and so cannot themselves be subject to critical scrutiny.[9] Only a mad person would try to prove that the world did – or did not – begin five minutes ago. For Pyrrhonian sceptics, that things seem to us as they do – at least at a given moment – cannot be challenged nor given any grounding. Montaigne, himself an admirer of the Greek Sceptics, argued that religious believers should "submit totally to the authority" of the church and follow "the beaten track" that it lays down for us. After all, for Pyrrhonian reasons, no rational case can be established *against* the church's authority.[10]

Montaigne's point also illustrates the intellectual or epistemic humility that the quietists recommend. This is the humility that requires people to admit to the limits of reason and human understanding, and to desist from elevating their own convictions over the seasoned judgements of long traditions of reflection and enquiry. In one form, it is the humility expressed in Wittgenstein's modest conception of philosophy as something that, rather than delineating reality, "consists in assembling reminders for particular purposes".[11]

Finally, of course, all these quietists value the tranquillity and equanimity that follow recovery from the "illness" and mental cramps that afflict those with a compulsion to engage in metaphysics. The three aims of his life that Montaigne had inscribed on his wall were "liberty, tranquillity, leisure". The suspension of judgement (*epoché*) recommended by the Greek Sceptics contributes to *ataraxia* – the freedom from disturbance which the wise person prizes above all else. The "fasting of the mind" urged by Zhuangzi – an "expulsion" of intellectual knowledge – enables people to experience "the presence of beings" in stillness.[12]

Certainly, there are metaphysical issues – the existence or otherwise of freedom of the will, for example – that can cause anxiety in those who struggle to resolve them. Such people may welcome a demonstration of the pointlessness of the struggle. But the concern with tranquillity of many of the figures I've mentioned goes far beyond the "peace" that a philosopher may enjoy after laying various issues to rest. For them, tranquillity or a close relative is at the very least a main objective of living well. It is a reward of a good life, not just of the abandonment of some intellectual struggles. It is, in effect, emancipation from what these figures perceive as the deeply flawed condition of humankind, for this is a condition marked not only by our many failings, but by discontent, anxiety and emotional turbulence.

These thinkers are philosophical quietists in the second of the senses of this expression I identified: they are proponents of certain, related views of the good life. I say "related", since the Stoic goal of *apatheia* (freedom from passion), the Epicurean and Pyrrhonian ideal of *ataraxia*, the "stillness" valued by the Daoists, and the Buddhist "sublime abode" of *upekkhā* (equanimity) are not identical. Nevertheless, they form a cluster of conceptions of one – and for some, *the* – goal of living well. For our present purposes, it is not necessary to decide which, if any, best achieves the quietist accommodation of pessimistic, misanthropic disquiet.

There existed, moreover, a broad consensus among these schools of thought on how the goals are to be achieved. Just as they did in the forms of quietism already discussed, the trio of acceptance, detachment and humility play leading parts. The Daoist sage submits to the gentle governance of the *dao*, and desists from "contending" with people and things. The wise Stoic, like Epictetus, should accept the way things are just as the good citizen accepts the laws of the state. This entails humility, as does the sceptics' rejection of dogmatism and bogus certainty. For Laozi, too, humility – never "putting oneself first" – is a "treasure".[13] Detachment from human affairs and from everything we are apt to grasp after and become attached to is, of course, a central teaching of the Buddha. It is a teaching that Zhuangzi would have endorsed: the good

Daoist will live "free of entanglements" and "lets go of the world".[14]

Some, but not all, of these thinkers thought that something further was required for the attainment of tranquillity, equanimity and the like – namely, philosophy. They are, therefore, philosophical quietists in the third of the senses I distinguished: they make a claim about the therapeutic role of philosophy in the good life. Epicurus, for example, held that a main obstacle to peace of mind was a fear of death that can be dispelled by a philosophical proof that "death is nothing".[15] The febrile, ever-anxious and competitive pursuit of knowledge, the Sceptics held, can be brought to an end by philosophical arguments demonstrating the impossibility of knowledge. Epictetus hoped to discourage people from the pursuit of power by showing that, really, a person can have power over nothing except his own mind.[16] And the Buddha, we know, held that equanimity and liberation are possible only for someone who understands the nature of suffering, its roots and the path to overcoming it.

On these conceptions, philosophy – the right sort, that is – is not some intellectual endeavour remote from life. Rather, it belongs integrally to a way of life in which tranquillity and equanimity are cultivated.[17] It is important to recognize this, for talk of tranquillity as a "goal" might suggest that it is simply a relaxed state of mind that could just as well be produced by diazepam or deep breathing. This, as we'll soon see, is a misleading suggestion.

I end this brief survey of philosophical quietisms with a point that recalls one that I made in Chapter 3. One reason, I proposed, for looking at ancient traditions was to loosen the modern conviction that the response to disquiet about the human condition must be to *do* something – to commit oneself to meliorative causes, to change the world, to save the planet, and so on. Advice to a young person with a negative perception of humankind to accept things, disengage and seek tranquillity is likely, these days, to be rejected out of hand. Well, it helps to remind ourselves that it was not always so. Only sixty years ago, as we'll see in the next chapter, young American hippies were lapping up such advice. In ancient times, such advice would have been commonplace, and many young people would have welcomed it as the voice of wisdom. Indeed, it was once no less obvious to reflective people that the good life was a quietist one than it is to people today that it is an energetic *via activa*.

IN A QUIETIST KEY

In this final section, I draw upon this ancient wisdom in order to articulate the aspirations of quietists, the desiderata on which they agree. I want to describe, one could say, what it is to live in a quietist key.

In at least three respects, the description will be relatively bland. First, it abstracts from the significant doctrinal differences among the forms of quietism encountered earlier in this chapter. For example, the aspirations I describe do not presuppose religious beliefs, like those of the Molinists. Second, it abstracts from differences over the interpretation of some central quietist notions – detachment and humility, for instance. Finally, I want the description to be at least putatively compatible with the diverse modes of living discussed in the next chapter. For these are ways regarded by their followers as faithful to the quietist dispensation, and they are at least prima facie in a quietist key.

Let's remind ourselves, before continuing, of the context in which I place quietism. Alongside other responses – amnesia, nihilism and activism – quietism accepts the pessimistic and misanthropic verdicts on humankind. It is a way of managing or accommodating the disquiet experienced by anyone who takes these verdicts seriously. For the same reasons as I gave when criticizing the other responses, the quietist also rejects them. Either, like amnesia, these responses ignore the verdicts or, like nihilism and activism, they combine lack of realism with exacerbation of human failings.

The quietist response is both more personal and more modest than those of the nihilist and activist. Its concern is not with obliterating humankind, radically improving the human condition, or changing the world. The quietist's concern is better described as one with care or cultivation of the self. The starting point is the first-personal question "How should I live in the light of the bleak vision of the human condition?" Care of the self does not mean that the quietist's focus is a purely "inner" or "private" one, directed at a self isolated from engagement with the world and other people. Quietists differ as to the kind and extent of such engagement, but none of them would, or indeed sensibly could, deny that self-cultivation requires it.

The quietist response to pessimism and misanthropy is more modest than its rivals in two ways. First, quietists accept that, except perhaps for some very remarkable people – quietist virtuosi, as it were – they are not going fully to realize their aspirations. Complete realization calls on capabilities – rigorous self-discipline, for example – that very few people possess. So, the modest and realistic quietist knows that he or she will at best approximate to realization of the aspirations. Second, quietists are well aware of the contingencies and vicissitudes to which human life is subject. Even the virtuosi need a lot of luck – the good fortune, for example, of having some wise teachers or living in times and places that allow for reflection and rational discussion. So, quietists will recognize that any success in pursuing their aspirations will be thanks, in considerable part, to circumstances beyond their control.

What, then, are the quietists' aspirations? What are the marks, the desiderata, of the good life as they understand it? First, they aspire to live as free as possible from unnecessary suffering – from the disturbance, perturbation, fears, anxiety, disappointments, frustrations, regrets, remorse and much else that figure in the pessimist's catalogue of the condition of most human beings. The aspiration is to live in tranquillity, equanimity and peace. It is, in effect, to live happily when this is understood, as it was by many ancients, primarily in terms of freedom from suffering. The quietist's life must therefore involve acceptance, to a significant degree, of how things are – an eschewal of the unrealistic desires that result in disappointment, reproach, anger, and so on. This in turn requires a certain detachment or disengagement – practical, emotional or both – from the business of everyday life most liable to cause anxiety and related types of suffering.

Next, quietists aspire to live without the failings and vices identified by the misanthrope – jealousy, vanity, hubris, greed, cruelty, hatred, contentiousness, and the rest. They aspire, in effect, to live virtuously, to exercise humility, equanimity, compassion, temperance and the like. After all, many virtues – most, perhaps – are best understood as "corrective", in the sense that they act as antidotes to corresponding vices.[18] Temperance, for instance, is the counter to greed, as is compassion to indifference or hardness of heart.

Third, quietists aspire to live, one might say, "in the truth".

This means, to begin with, that they aim to be free from the illusions, delusions, prejudices, biases, culpable ignorance, self-deception and much else that distort people's perception, understanding and judgement. In short, they aspire to live without the epistemic failings that are entrenched in human life. Harder to make precise, but of great importance to many quietists, is also aspiration to a life that accords with the way of things and is guided by it. Daoists, Buddhists, Christians, Stoics and Epicureans may have different understandings of the world, but for all of them a good life is consonant with, and submits to, the truth of how things ultimately are. (The importance of this point emerges in Chapter 9.)

I have listed three quietist aspirations, but it is essential to recognize that they are not independent of one another. The aspiration to live in tranquillity and happiness entails the aspiration to live without failings and vices for two reasons, one obvious and the other less so. The obvious one is that it is these failings that are responsible for much of the unnecessary suffering from which the quietist aspires to be free.

The less obvious reason is that tranquillity and happiness are not inner mental states that happen, fortuitously, to be produced by exercising the virtues. Quietists prize moments of calm and contentment as much as the next person, but this is not what they aspire to. As Aristotle made clear when discussing *eudaimonia* – often translated as "happiness" – this is constituted by living virtuously and is not something separate from it that virtue happens to cause.[19] The equanimous person, for example, will enjoy the periods of calm and self-assurance that their way of living enables. More importantly, however, this equanimity is manifested in a manner of judging and assessing, making decisions and expressing opinions, responding to people and treating them – a manner marked by absence of bias and prejudice, sober reasoning, and mindful attentiveness. Compassion is not having a bleeding heart and becoming tearful over the suffering of some creature, but a virtue exercised in helping or comforting it. To aspire to tranquillity, therefore, is necessarily to aspire to a life informed by various virtues.

The aspiration to reduce or eliminate one's failings, meanwhile, entails the third aspiration, to live "in the truth" – again, for a more and a less obvious reason. The first reason is that some of these failings are epistemic ones that distract from, or occlude access to, truth. Self-deception, dogmatism, prejudice and culpable ignorance are just some of these failings. A virtue like equanimity, we just saw, is as much an emancipation from failings like these as from greed and vanity.

The second, and more interesting, reason is that, as Aristotle explained, a full exercise of virtue is possible only for a person who "acquires understanding" and practical wisdom.[20] Buddhists, Stoics and others would all agree that the virtue of, say, compassion does not consist in being good-hearted and feeling sympathetic. It requires judgement as to whether the sympathy is deserved and, if it is, intelligent reflection on the best course of action. This point registers part of what the ancients intended by a doctrine on which they nearly all agreed – the unity of wisdom and virtue.

These, then, are the quietist's aspirations and some of the connections between them. It is the attempt to meet these aspirations that constitutes the quietist way of accommodating the disquiet occasioned by agreement with pessimism and misanthropy. I accommodate the disquiet by my living as well as I can. This means leading a life that is, to a degree, emancipated from the human condition – from the practices, processes and structures of ordinary human existence that are productive of great suffering and suffused with human failings. (The rhetoric of a transcendence of the human condition is familiar among ancient quietists – the Buddha, for example, or the Desert Fathers.) The good quietist is something of an exile, like someone who emigrates from a country famed for its injustice, cruelty and corruption.

For the reasons I gave earlier, my account of what it is to live in a quietist key is schematic, bland even. One of these reasons was a reluctance to exclude any of several different ways of living that might reasonably be regarded as quietist in tone. We'll encounter some of these in the next chapter.

5

Modes of quietism

EGOISM?

There is more, as we saw at the end of the last chapter, that we want to know about quietists – notably, the modes or strategies of living consistent with their aspirations. But we already know enough about quietism to consider a charge that is sometimes made against it – that of egoism. This is a complaint that, historically, has often been levelled – by, for example, both Mahāyāna Buddhists and Confucians against the Theravāda monk whose goal is to become enlightened, or by the Catholic Church against the Molinists for their disregard of "good works". I don't want to enter into the intricacies of these particular cases, but they indicate that there are two grounds for the egoism charge – quietism's eschewal of meliorist, activist ambitions and its focus on the first personal question of how to live. Neither of these grounds are sound.

The critic of quietism argues, first, that quietists demonstrate their egoism and self-centredness by asking "How should *I* live in response to the pessimistic, misanthropic judgement of the human condition?". The question implies, critics allege, that, for the quietist, it is only his or her own life that is of concern. Well, it is true that the question is self-directed and that self-cultivation, or care of the self, is quiet-ism's primary focus. But this does not imply that the quietist life is selfish, self-centred, or egoistic in the sense that these terms have in ordinary discourse. Quietists, that is, do not ignore the interests and well-being of other people or crea-tures except in so far as these bear upon their own advantage.

For the quietist, selfishness – and its many neighbours, including greed, vanity, insensitivity, and lack of charity – are failings or vices. They are dispositions one should try to be rid of, not to indulge. In exercising virtues, the quietist's motivation is not self-advantage, but to counter the failings responsible for much of our suffering and, in doing so, to live a good life. The critic is guilty of confusing self-cultivation and self-concern with self-advantage and self-centredness. Put differently, there is confusion between self-reflective atten-tion to the I or ego and exclusive preoccupation with one's own interest – egoism, that is. That, as noted in the Prologue, the "the point of entry for ethical reflection" is a concern for one's self does not entail that the point of exit is a set of self-serving precepts.

It is true, of course, that quietists do not think that the way to counter failings and vices is through commitment to large moral and political causes. They are likely to agree with George Eliot's remark, in part quoted earlier, that where there is "growing good", this is likely to be the result of the many small "unhistoric acts" of people who lived a largely "hidden life", and "rest in unvisited tombs". But to regard eschewal of activism as a criterion of egoism is possible only in a morally myopic culture that has forgotten the existence of the many virtues – including humility, honesty, loyalty, temperance and forbearance – that are absent from muscular attempts to change the world. This is a culture – like our contemporary one, in fact – in which enthusiasm for big and noisy causes eclipses attention to, among much else, how people should conduct their personal relationships with one another.

It is true as well that quietists regard their personal happiness and tranquillity as legitimate aspirations. To the complaint that this in itself is a mark of selfishness, there are a number of replies. First, an ethic in which concern for one's own well-being is denounced sounds masochistic and is anyway one to which only a very tiny number of people could genuinely subscribe. This doesn't, of course, prevent people from mouthing support for it and ridiculing those people who, for example, focus instead on having a decent job, making a happy marriage, and raising a family. But it is, nevertheless, a pie-in-the-sky ethic.

Second, as we saw in the previous chapter, the happiness and tranquillity aspired to by quietists are not independent of the virtues. To live happily requires, other things being equal, the exercise of such virtues as compassion, equanimity and "empathetic joy" – to list some main Buddhist virtues. The life of the hard-hearted, hateful, jealous, resentful, angry, vengeful person is not a happy and tranquil one. When the Buddha said that "protecting oneself, one protects others; protecting others, one protects oneself", he was emphasizing that enlightened and responsible ways of engaging with the world and with other people are integral to a person's own good.[1]

Quietists will, naturally, encounter situations where a difficult choice has to be made between one's own good and that of others, or between the good of someone close and that of distant strangers. But, then, so does everyone. Leading a good life is not a simple matter: there is no algorithm for making decisions. Appeals to general moral principles such as the

Golden Rule, the principle of utility, or the categorical imperative, either yield no answers at all or pat, mechanical ones of
which those who confront real moral dilemmas are rightly
wary. One wonders, too, if iron commitment to activist causes
is not sometimes a strategy for evading dilemmas and escaping the need for moral reflection. When quietists choose what
they see as their own good over that of others, the charge of
selfishness may sometimes be appropriate, but often it won't
be. For example, even if one is critical of them, "selfish" is quite
the wrong word to describe those disciples of the Buddha or
Christ who, in order to seek enlightenment or salvation, left
their families and friends.

With the complaint of egoism against quietists rejected,
let's now look at some of the ways that those with quietist
aspirations might conduct their lives.

DROPPING OUT

In Chapter 2, we encountered the type of misanthrope that
Kant called "the Enemy of Mankind", but he recognized – and
had more sympathy for – a second type, "the Fugitive from
Mankind".[2] Depressed by the scale of human vices and failings, this figure withdraws from society out of fear, including
especially a fear of falling in with the ways of society, and of
becoming thereby morally corrupted. A more apt and evoca-
tive term than "fugitive", in the present context, would be
"dropout". Those paradigmatic dropouts – American hippies
of the 1960s – wanted not only to "decontaminate" themselves, but to get out of the cities and lead quiet lives in small
communities well away from the business and tumult of
modern society.

Most of the hippies were without any activist ambitions. Avoid the whole "external political drama", and eschew "mass movements", advised their guru, the psychologist Timothy Leary.[3] Don't try to reform society, advised another leading figure: "just leave it and go someplace else".[4] The focus should, instead, be on cultivation of one's soul, "natural energies" and body – something feasibly to achieve in rural environments with the help of "essential friends", plenty of "sexual union", and drugs. No work would be done in these little communities beyond what was necessary for sustaining a simple, frugal lifestyle, and children would be kept away from school – that incubator in which the young were indoctrinated into the values of an acquisitive and mendacious culture.

Dropping out did not begin, of course, in the 1960s, and among the many dropouts in history, different goals or orientations can be found. The most familiar, perhaps, is that of "lotus-eaters", as we might call them. Here, the goal is to find peace in the form of quiet, benign and abiding pleasures. This requires extraction from the situations, of which the everyday social world as well as work environments are full, that encourage the exercise of our moral failings. The hope, unlike that of the "amnesiacs" in Chapter 2, is not to forget the parlous condition of humankind. Instead, it is to cope with the disquiet this causes by keeping one's hands clean, by tranquil withdrawal from modern human life. In Tennyson's poem, "The Lotos-Eaters", Odysseus' sailors, wanting to remain on the island whose contented natives ingest the lotus flowers, do not aim to erase memories of the sorrows and evils of the world, but to accommodate them within a life of "dreamful ease".

Other dropouts, however, have been motivated less by a desire for pleasurable ease than for a space in which to engage in reflection. Their negative perception of humankind is focused less on greed and other moral failings than on those directly responsible for myopic or distorted understanding – on prejudices, false consciousness, and ideologies that occlude recognition of truths. Dropping out of modern social life is, for them, liberation from what corrupts thought and judgement. Or – as with many artists and poets who have dropped out – the aim may be to preserve, like "The Hermit of Treig" in the celebrated film of that name, an integrity hard to maintain in a society whose cultural scene is dominated by commercial interests, subject to ideological fads, and hospitable to bigotry and moral policing.

I could go on listing types of dropouts, but we already know enough to ask the question of the aptness of dropping out as a strategy for realizing quietist aspirations. It would be wrong – despite the silliness and worse of many of the "flower-power" generation – to dismiss it out of hand as a strategy for achieving tranquillity, a degree of moral cleanliness, and an unprejudiced awareness and sensibility. These are achievements that all quietists want to incorporate into their lives.

Ironically, however, it was the prophet of dropping out, Timothy Leary, who articulated the principal problems with the strategy. Referring to the man whom he regarded as the greatest of all dropouts, the Buddha, Leary stresses that the dropout's path is a "demanding, arduous road". It's easy enough to play-act – to take off for a few months to the desert with congenial friends, mescalin, and some Hermann Hesse books – but extremely difficult to turn dropping out into an abiding way of life. Few of us are equipped, materially or psychologically, to undertake a serious commitment to live outside of society, and even fewer to sustain this commitment in the long term. Hardly any of the flower-power dropouts, unsurprisingly, stayed in the desert, eventually returning instead to cities they had left.

It is this return – this "coming back down" – that is the second problem Leary identifies. Having told his followers to "turn on" and drop out, he then instructs them to "tune in" once they "drop back" – as nearly all of them will – into the "social drama".[5] But this invites the question, on which Leary is disappointingly silent, of how the erstwhile dropouts do "tune in" – how, that is, they play their parts, in a quietist spirit, in the drama they once renounced. How, having been told that peace, goodness and understanding require abdication from society, can they hope to pursue them on their return from self-imposed exile?

"NOT DOING" AND "HUMANENESS"

The reason that dropping out and lotus-eating so readily invite the "quietist" label is the image they conjure up of people not doing anything. How much quieter can life get than that? There is a famous Chinese term, *wu wei*, that means "not doing" and has an important place in Daoist thought. It is a term worth thinking about when trying to locate a quietist way of life that does not entail the degree of disengagement from society chosen by the dropout.[6]

Not even the dedicated lotus-eater literally does nothing, and the Daoist exemplars of *wu wei* are certainly not lazy couch potatoes. On the contrary, they are typically craftsmen and other people who exercise skills, such as butchers, gardeners and swimmers. "Activity cannot be avoided", Zhuangzi reminds us:[7] what can be avoided, however, is laboured, effortful or frenetic action. The skilled wood carver, for example, exhibits *wu wei* when, instead of imposing a preconceived plan on the block of wood, he attends to and responds to the natural grain of the wood. More generally, *wu wei* is exercised when people act flexibly and spontaneously rather than mechanically follow rules, and when they are ready to adjust their goals according to circumstances instead of pursuing them come what may. "Not doing" is a relaxed and supple style of doing, free from the constraints and frets that make so much of our activity a chore. The Daoist wood carvers, butchers and swimmers are responsive and serene in their work: like the skilled swimmer Zhuangzi describes, they too "go with the flow", as we nowadays say.

The *Daodejing* advises the sage ruler to "do the not doing", for then nothing is left undone.[8] *Wu wei*, then, is not restricted to dealings with materials – meat, wood, water, plants – but is exercised as well in dealings with people. The ruler who follows Laozi's advice imposes his will as little as possible on his subjects, avoids contention and eschews the use of force. Those he rules are barely aware of having a ruler. And the rest of us, in ordinary life, should in these respects emulate the ruler. Our relations with one another, ideally, are marked by spontaneity and an avoidance of confrontation.

This requires a degree of ironic detachment from the everyday business of life, without which it is impossible to rise above and appraise the rules, conventions, purposes and ambitions that threaten to dictate one's own life and to rigidify one's relations with others. It is just such an ironic stance towards their work as government officials that was taken, one imagines, by Chinese poets like Wang Wei and Tao Yuanming, whose verses celebrate their intermittent escapes from the "dust-filled trap" of the city to "an old forest home".[9]

Wu wei is possible only for those who do not overreach themselves, recognize the limits to their ability to impose themselves on the world and each other, and confine their practices to those in which they are skilled and effective. And it is possible only for those who are suspicious of the dogmas and unbending conventions that dictate and restrict our practices. For "not doers", the principal kind of knowledge to cultivate is not theoretical or propositional, but the unspoken "know-how" manifested in skilful dealings with the world and one's fellow human beings.

People adept in *wu wei* are attractive quietist figures. Calm and collected, at ease in their skilful practice, they display a tranquillity denied to most people. Confident in their skills, they are nevertheless modest about their capacity to change the world, and sceptical about the effectiveness of muscular activism. Ironic detachment, rather than enthusiasm, is their stance towards ambitious collective goals. The know-how they display indicates an accurate and implicit understanding of people and things. In addition to enjoying tranquillity, therefore, they also exhibit an array of quietist virtues, moral and epistemic alike.

May we conclude, then, that the "not doer" – the adept in *wu wei* – leads a life that realizes the quietist aspirations? To see why the answer cannot be a simple affirmative, it is helpful to look at some standard criticisms levelled by Confucians of their Daoist contemporaries. One of the charges – to the effect that Daoists are "amoral" and "selfish" – is wayward, for the same reasons that such charges against quietism in general are. Certainly it is wrong to ignore the moral setting of the Daoist advocacy of *wu wei*. While Zhuangzi's writing is amusing and buoyant, it also conveys a "dark despair and a pitiless wisdom".[10] Human life is characterized by greed, lust

71

for power, ambition, love of change for its own sake, and fascination with the latest fads and technological contrivances. Above all, it is marked by febrile "busyness", an urge constantly to be "doing something", achieving some aim, chasing some dream, with the result that people are tossed about in a social and economic maelstrom. Most people, for the whole of their lives, are unable to stay still and "turn back. How sad!".[11]

Wu wei, then, is not lotus-eating self-indulgence, but a way of extracting oneself, and those one is able to influence, from a form of existence that is not only full of suffering and anxiety, but infested by human vices and failings. That said, there is a more moderate Confucian criticism that is more persuasive than the blunt charge of egoism and amoralism. Nothing in my sketch of "not doers" dispels the thought that they are, so to speak, rather cold fish. Cool, calm, ironically detached from much of the business of life, their moral virtues, like humility, are not ones that, in any obvious way at least, benefit other beings. They do not include, for example, compassion, benevolence, fidelity, familial piety and respect. (Confucians are fond of citing an anecdote about Zhuangzi cheerfully playing a drum immediately after his wife's death.) Nor, from my sketch, does it appear that *wu wei* involves such ingredients of the good life as a sense of beauty and appreciation of art and nature. There are, then, aspects of the life to which quietists aspire that do not figure in that of the adept in *wu wei*.

What is missing I shall call "humaneness". This word is sometimes used to translate the important Confucian term, *ren*, that names the quality of life to which good Confucians aspire. (Other translations on offer include "benevolence", "human-heartedness", and "inner moral force"). Whether or not "humaneness" captures the concept of *ren* is not, however, important: it is a useful term for identifying what – or so it seemed to Confucian critics of Daoism like Xunzi – is missing from the moral repertoire of the "not doer".

For a start, "humane" familiarly describes compassionate and benevolent attitudes. A humane person treats the animals in their care kindly and sympathizes with the suffering of a neighbour. As such examples suggest, humaneness is exercised in particular contexts and, as it were, "locally". "Humane" isn't the appropriate word to describe people fired up by a sense of global injustice or on the march in order to save the planet. Humane persons confine their interventions to ones that stand a good chance of being effective, hence to what they can do "here and now and in little things", as Heidegger put it.[12] It is humaneness that Count Bezukhov, in *War and Peace*, discovers when he becomes disillusioned with his grandiose ambitions to establish "the rights of man", put an end to serfdom and the like. Recognizing that these blinded him to the plight of particular people and creatures in particular situations, he decides to focus on little things, on what he is able to help with or put right. "How splendid!", he declares.[13]

"Humane" also suggests a further quietist aspiration that, it seemed, was missing from "not doing". The humane studies, as Renaissance authors called them, were those that were believed, rightly or not, to be edifying. The humane person, as imagined by these writers, was certainly concerned, among other things, to appreciate the beauty of works of art, the bodies of men, women and animals, and the natural world. The point was not simply, or at all, decadently to enjoy "delicious sensations", for beauty, properly understood, is inseparable from virtue. Not only, as the quintessential "Renaissance Man", Leon Battista Alberti, put it, is appreciation of beauty

73

the "best indication of a most perfect mind", but beauty is expressive of virtues – humility, courage, compassion, or whatever – that shine forth, as it were, in beautiful faces, say, or paintings.[14] Humane sensitivity to beauty is an ingredient in the life of the good quietist, therefore, for it enables a retreat or relief from the vulgarity, glitter and ugliness – moral as much as aesthetic – of much of the human world.

QUIETISM AND DISQUIET

The quietist way of life most consonant with quietist aspirations might, then, be described as humane *wu wei*. Flexible and spontaneous, disentangled from the busyness of the world, uncontending, distanced from rigid rules and conventions, disencumbered of dogma and prejudice, compassionate, modest in their moral interventions, and appreciative of beauty, humane "not doers" appear close to realizing the quietist aspirations. Tranquillity and equanimity, freedom from a wide range of human failings, and true understanding of things look to be the benefits of this strategy for living.

But doubts creep in. Can the form of quietism we have arrived at fully accommodate and manage the disquiet that pessimism and misanthropy arouse? In order to do so, does quietism require to be supplemented, modified, or put into a larger context? Two reservations will be felt by at least some of those who experience this disquiet.

The first is whether humane "not doers" are, after all, "in the truth" to which quietists aspire. Granted, they are free from various prejudices, dogmas and illusions that obstruct understanding of people and the world. But this is not sufficient to allay a fear that one's whole way of responding to disquiet may be askew and unwarranted. What is to prevent quietists waking up one morning and finding themselves without any confidence in the prioritization of tranquillity and quiet virtues like humility and equanimity? This is a fear all the more likely to arise in a cultural, moral environment where such virtues are derided or ignored in favour of more global and muscular activist goals.

This kind of anxiety can only deepen or amplify the disquiet that a dark perception of humankind invites, and is one that several quietist thinkers have articulated. Zhuangzi writes that the understanding required to know "what is to be done by the human ... can be in the right only by virtue of a relation of dependence on something, one that is peculiarly unfixed".[15] Kierkegaard holds that what he calls "the ethical way of life" – a way with a pronounced quietist tone – is fragile and liable to "despair" because it is not "grounded" in anything beyond itself.[16]

Remarks like these indicate the thought that, if a life is to be "in the truth", it is not sufficient for it to be free from prejudices, delusions and so on. It must also be consonant with, or "grounded" in, something that provides a measure for how we should live – something to which our lives are answerable. Zhuangzi and Kierkegaard were in the happy position of knowing what this something is – the *dao* (The Way), and the transcendent "Power" of the Christian God, respectively. Disquiet, for them, is resolved by recognizing the consonance of the quietist life with a way or power on which we are dependent. Not everyone, of course, is a Daoist or a Christian, but this does not gainsay the possibility that something like the religious sense of Zhuangzi and Kierkegaard is required for quietism to be perceived as "in the truth". This is a theme we return to in Chapter 9.

75

I'll be turning, first, to another concern about the sufficiency of the quietist response to disquiet. The concern, this time, is not with the truthfulness of the quietist life, but with its capacity to satisfy an emotional need that is often experienced in close conjunction with disquiet. I shall call it the need for *refuge* – refuge, that is, from the human world or condition, a "place" in which safety and comfort is found, and where one does not feel alien. The concern, then, is that the quietist way of living, as so far characterized, in terms of humane "not doing", does not, in itself, provide such a place: it does not offer refuge.

6

Refuge

THE RHETORIC OF REFUGE

Michel de Montaigne, whom we encountered earlier as a representative of pessimism and misanthropy, wrote that while we should, by all means, have wives, children and property, we should also "set aside a room, just for ourselves, at the back of the shop". For it is there that we may establish "our true liberty, our principal solitude and asylum".[1] He is advising us that, to lead a good and contented life, a person requires refuge, a place set apart from even the more pleasant and laudable occupations of everyday life.

The frequency of references to a need for refuge among those whose judgement on humankind is negative, several of whom we've already met, is striking. Montaigne's remark reminds one of his compatriot, Pascal's, famous comment that "man's unhappiness springs from ... his incapacity to stay quietly in one room ... at home".[2] Although famous, this is usually misunderstood to mean that it is essential to be able to be alone and enjoy solitude. Pascal's actual point is that staying at home is a refuge from "quarrels, passions, risky, often ill-conceived actions" and the pressure constantly to indulge in "diversions".

Here are a couple of more recent examples. In W. G. Sebald's book, *Austerlitz*, a *schwarzsehend* character – reflecting to an extent the author's own perspective – describes how, in a decadent world, he keeps himself apart from current affairs, avoids newspapers, and creates "a kind of quarantine" in order to "maintain his existence".[3] Aldous Huxley writes of "the urge to escape", and to seek refuge from, a world in which most people lead lives that, when not "painful", are "monotonous, poor and limited", except when indulging in "orgies and intoxicants".[4]

The rhetoric of refuge is especially pronounced in the texts of religions which maintain that, unless illuminated by faith, the human condition is a parlous and perilous one. The penultimate chapter of the *Quran* enjoins the faithful to "seek refuge in the Lord of the daybreak from the evil of whatever He has created" (113.1-2), and seeking refuge from Satan is part of Moslems' daily prayers. Christian authors use similar terminology. St Ambrose of Milan, for example, instructs us to "take refuge from this world" in order that we may, "in spirit", be "present to the Lord".[5] Martin Luther, in one of his many hymns, famously assured Christians that their God was "a mighty fortress" (*Ein feste Burg*) in which they will find protection.

It is in the texts and practices of Buddhism, perhaps, where the idea of refuge is most prominent. A practising Buddhist is someone who has "gone for refuge", and regularly recites a verse that attests to trust in the "threefold refuge" (*tisarana*). This trio consists of the Buddha, his *dhamma* or teaching, and the *sangha*, the community of "noble" persons, predominantly monks, who are already, or on the way to becoming, enlightened. As the celebrated German-born Buddhist monk and writer, Nyanaponika, explains, the importance of these refuges becomes apparent once one sees clearly "the hard and cruel face of the world". Life is "a vast ocean of suffering" and "this world of ours ... [is] such a place of danger and misery that there is a need for taking refuge".[6]

Here, then, are examples of the widespread rhetoric of refuge adopted by a wide variety of figures who share a dark, negative perception of human existence. In fact, the rhetoric is wider that it might at first seem, once we include in it references to such close relatives of refuges as asylums, sanctuaries and places of voluntary exile. This rhetoric, while it is still heard today, is less prevalent than it once was. In our present bright-siding, boosterish culture, the idea that we require refuge from ordinary human life is liable to be dismissed or ignored. When the word "refuge" is used rhetorically, it is often in jokey, cynical remarks modelled on Dr Johnson's "Patriotism is the last refuge of a scoundrel" – for example, "Jazz is the last refuge of the untalented".

It is clear from the examples I've already given of a serious rhetoric of refuge that very different things or places may be regarded as refuges – a backroom, God, a religious community, a body of teachings, self-isolation, and so on.[7] A quick trawl through the literature would soon yield references to many other putative refuges from the everyday world – natural environments, gardens, music, love, sex, scholarship, solitary huts, and the Jewish Sabbath, for instance. These examples also show that many of the places of refuge are so only in extended or metaphorical senses of the terms. Music, sex and love are not places of refuge in the literal sense of physical spaces that afford protection.

In fact, none of the refuges alluded to – not even Montaigne's backroom – should be thought of as consisting simply in a physical space or structure, in something, that is, that could be defined geographically or geometrically. As Montaigne explains, the asylum he cherishes is not a space enclosed by four walls and a ceiling, but the "conversation with [himself]" that – through excluding noise, bustle and chatter – the backroom makes possible.[8] Or consider the garden to which a Daoist poet escapes from the dust and grime of the city – this is not a refuge in the way it is for a rabbit escaping from a pursuing fox, a place of physical security. For the poet, the walls, gate, trees and paths of the garden are the context or environment for relaxation, reflection, enjoyment and the leisure to write. It is these in which the poet finds refuge.

Similar remarks could be made about a monastery: this is not a refuge for those who are there on retreat in the manner it might be for a prisoner on the run from the baying dogs of his pursuers. For those on retreat, the building is the context or setting for the temporary refuge they find in meditation, simple menial tasks, quiet conversation and prayer.

This is not to say that the physical character or design of the building – or the garden, or the backroom – doesn't matter. On the contrary, this may be essential to its aptness for providing an environment for refuge. Nor is it necessary to register the point I've been making by a pedantic denial that the monasteries, gardens, rooms, huts or homes themselves are places of refuge. The important thing is to bear in mind that, strictly, the refuge is not the physical structure, but what this structure enables in response to the need for refuge of those who enter it. The sense of metaphor at work when we speak of a garden or a room as a refuge may not be as strong as when love or music are described as refuges. But in none of these cases – the first two as much as the second pair – is the reference being made to refuges in the original and primary sense of the word.

It is important, though, that the primary sense should guide and constrain the rhetorical, figurative talk of refuge if such talk is to be cogent and effective.

THE NEED FOR REFUGE

Why do so many people, including quietists, who experience disquiet at the human condition reach for the vocabulary of refuge? That they speak of a need for refuge suggests that there is something insufficient, something missing, in the quietist response to disquiet as described in the previous chapter. The quietist way of life, to recall, was characterized as "humane *wu wei*". This was a combination of a certain detachment or disentanglement from the busyness, strictures and vices of everyday life, the adoption of modest and realistic moral aspirations, and the cultivation of understanding, sensibility and appreciation. This quietist way of life is intended to achieve tranquillity and contentment in response to the disquiet occasioned by the perception of "the hard and cruel face of the world", to recall Nyanaponika's phrase.

So what is it that is missing from the quietist strategy for managing disquiet that the rhetoric of refuge indicates? And does it show how quietism must be supplemented if disquiet is to be not just coped with, but relieved?

A poem of Goethe's contains these lines:

> ... [W]e're thrown upon the world,
> Thousands of waves wash round us without cease,
> ...
> Our senses have a strange, tumultuous power,
> And in the turmoil find no place to stay.[9]

81

Expressed here is the thought that it is not sufficient merely to cope with and accommodate to the everyday human world into which we are all thrown. We need, as well, a place set apart from this world into which to retreat. In the words of another poet, Wordsworth, this world is oppressively "too much with us", so that refuge from it must be sought in "Nature", with which we have, he writes, become "out of tune".[10]

What is being proposed here is not the way of the drop-out, whom I characterized as intending to live permanently outside of ordinary human society. The point, rather, is that the quietist who manages to accommodate to that world will sometimes require more than this accommodation – "another place", in effect, tangential to it into which to retreat. Like the refugee in the literal sense, who flees to another place rather than put up with staying where he or she was, so the quietist must at times seek another place instead of just getting by in the world the person has been "thrown upon". That world really is "too much with us" to put up with all the time.

The "other place" in which refuge is sought provides relief from disquiet in two ways. As a place set apart from everyday human affairs, it affords liberation, however fleeting, from the presence of the suffering, cruelty, pettiness, vanity and other aspects of human existence that invite the pessimistic and misanthropic verdicts which occasion disquiet. For a while, at least, disquiet, while not made to vanish, no longer colours experience. Leopardi wrote that once "the misanthrope withdraws from society ... he loses his misanthropy".[11] That may be right if what he means is that, during the withdrawal, the person's thoughts, actions and moods are not suffused with misanthropic disquiet, and an opportunity exists for repair.

Refuge offers relief in a second way. Leading a quietist life in the midst of everyday human affairs is not easy.

82

Maintaining a certain ironic distance from one's activities, for example, can be difficult in the face of the pressures on being more involved and committed. The quietist seeks tranquillity, but this is threatened by the sorts of work in which people are typically compelled to engage. Skill, effort and self-discipline are required to maintain detachment, but their exercise may then itself pose a threat to tranquillity. Consider, for example, the self-discipline required to leave behind or keep switched off one's smart phone. A refuge is, in part, a place where, freed from everyday pressures and temptations, a person does not have to struggle for detachment and equanimity. Zhuangzi noted that those who are "truly at ease" do not need to aim at peace and tranquillity as targets.[12] Refuges provide the possibility of – the ambience for – being truly at ease.

As these remarks indicate, a refuge offers more than escape and relief from something. The refugee who flees from one country to another expects or hopes that the second one will be better than the first. If it is just as poverty-stricken or war-torn, for example, there would be no point to the flight. Likewise, people who seek refuge from the world of disquiet are also seeking a place that is better in various respects than that world. It is a place that they might envision as more innocent and clean, as it were, than the everyday world. Or as one where they hope to find a beauty that is missing from their glitzy, vulgar everyday environments. Or perhaps they find the place to be more ordered and rational than the "tumultuous", hurly-burly existence from which refuge is sought.

Men and women who go on retreat to a monastery, for example, often express delight in the simple routines, order and regularity that obtain there, in welcome contrast to the febrile busyness they have briefly left behind.[13] In Jean-Paul Sartre's novel, *Nausea*, a striking passage describes how the "nausea" that the main protagonist, Roquentin, continually experiences at the meaningless, utterly contingent world around him ceases when listening to a record of the jazz standard, "Some of these Days". "I am *in* the music", Roquentin feels, and he recognizes the "necessity" of the notes following one another, the transparent meaning of each phrase in relation to the whole, the clear direction of the song towards its ending. The music is Roquentin's refuge, disjoined from the world that nauseates him.[14]

There are other things that refugees, in the literal sense, typically hope to find in the places to which they flee that have echoes in the quietist's need for "another place". The refugee may, for example, hope to discover freedoms – political and religious, say – that have been suppressed in the country fled from. Likewise, quietists and others who share a negative perception of their society's mode of life are acutely aware of the pressures and constraints that this mode imposes. We noted, earlier, for example, the imperative in many modern societies to "achieve" or to "be whatever you want to be", however unsuited you are to being what you want to be. The entry into a refuge – a natural environment, perhaps, or a musical work – is an escape from such pressures, and an act of freedom, for the refuge is a place where the only constraints are ones freely submitted to. The responsible backpacker roams freely, but accepts that she must not damage the flowers by the side of the path. The serious listener has chosen what record to play, but will, like Roquentin, submit to the "necessity" of the music, sensitive to its form and meaning.

And, of course, a refuge, unlike many of the places from which refugees wish to flee, is a place that one is free to leave. The same is true of the refuges sought by quietists. Indeed, the sojourns in the places where they find refuge are not seen as permanent, but to be entered and exited as one chooses. The backpacker returns from the mountains, though she may well go back to them next year. The music that's being listened to comes to an end, but the record can be put on the turntable again tomorrow.

A distressing feature of life in postwar Communist countries, humorously exposed in the novels of Milan Kundera, was its unpredictability. One didn't know when there would be a knock on the door, or whether a joke one had told would have serious repercussions for one's family. It was difficult, impossible even, to conduct one's life with confidence and trust. This was a main reason for people, like Kundera himself, to find refuge elsewhere. Similarly, quietists who have discovered refuge from the everyday human world find in it a place where they know their way around – where there is a certain predictability that enables them to conduct themselves with confidence and trust. With these comes a certain hope for the future.

A mountain range or a musical work may, of course, have its surprises – a new vista from the ridge, a sudden crescendo. But the experienced, skilled backpacker or listener expects and welcomes such surprises. They are budgeted for, and constitute part of the enjoyment of the place. They are quite unlike the unpredictable, unpleasant happenings and actions, constantly encountered in human affairs, that are impossible to cater for in advance. A refuge invites serenity, not because it is necessarily a quiet place in which little happens, but because of trust in one's ability to understand, cope with, and appropriately respond to what happens. Climbers and swimmers, for example, attest to the calm they experience even on narrow ridges or in waters that pose dangers. Not only are these dangers that they have chosen to risk but, unlike the menaces and hazards faced in the business of life, they are not the products of machination, ambition, jealousy and other human failings. The dangers, one might say, are innocent.

QUIETISM AND REFUGE

I have been arguing that quietism, as characterized in Chapter 5 – in terms of humane practices and sensibilities, detachment and ironic distance, and "not doing" – is insufficient as a response to pessimism, misanthropy and the mood of disquiet that they bring with them. Quietism, so understood, needs to be supplemented or enriched by finding refuge. A refuge is "another place" that affords scope for freedom, a promise of retreat from everyday busyness, and a prospect of tranquillity and happiness that exceed what is available in the world from which refuge is sought.

A way of seeing why quietism, unsupplemented, is insufficient as a response – incapable, in fact, of meeting the aspirations of quietists – is to appreciate that, in large part, the quietist strategy is a negative one. It emphasizes such goals as the absence of anxiety. It advises detachment and disengagement. It recommends that we should not be constrained by dogma, ideology and fashion. Some of the main, humane virtues it admires, like humility, take the form of refraining from the vices, like vanity, to which they run counter.

These are, of course, important merits of a strategy that responds to disquiet, but it remains one that does not satisfy a yearning for something more "positive". Earlier, I wrote of a need for a retreat from the everyday world that goes beyond the quietist aim of detachment from it. Equally, there is a need for something more fulfilling and satisfying than the quietist life, unsupplemented, provides. A refuge offers this something more "positive". Within a refuge, people experience innocence, order, beauty, freedom, or confidence in ways they typically do not in the places from which they have escaped. When inside their refuge, they are more likely to find fulfilment and happiness.

The quietist's hope was adequately to respond to disquiet. When describing the strategy in Chapter 5, the talk was of "coping with", "managing", or "accommodating to" disquiet. When talking of refuge, however, the language is more upbeat. Experience is no longer coloured or suffused by disquiet. Disquiet is, in effect, temporarily overcome or relieved. When taking refuge, the world – the space of the refuge, at least – waxes rather than wanes, to recall Wittgenstein's remark on the world and the mood of the happy man.

It matters little whether we stick with the description of the quietist from the previous chapter, or now build into it a search for and discovery of refuge. On the first option, quietism must be judged a failure in meeting its own aspirations. On the second, the prospects of quietism – now that it incorporates the finding of refuge – are more promising. It will be linguistically less clumsy to talk of quietism *tout court* rather than of quietism-supplemented-by-the-finding-of-refuge. It just needs remembering that, from now on, references to quietism are to this enriched concept, not to the earlier and leaner one.

Disquiet can never be expelled from the life of someone who endorses and, unlike the amnesiac, remains mindful of the pessimist's and the misanthrope's verdict on the human condition. Genuinely to endorse it is to be subject to disquiet. The question now is whether, to the maximum extent possible, quietism as now understood is able to give relief from disquiet. To address the question, let's consider the kind of places that, more than any other, have been turned to for refuge from a disquieting world. The kind in question is natural places.

7

Nature as refuge 1: "Another place"

My focus in this and the following chapter is on the refuge from the human world afforded by natural environments. Why this focus? Why exclude other types of possible refuge? One answer is that it doesn't exclude these others for, as we'll see, it is partly through their association or adjacence with nature that other places are often sought as refuges. Another answer is that, from page one, human relationships with nature have been an important theme of this book. It was with a walker's depression at the devastation of a landscape that the book began, and "eco-misanthropy" was a prominent topic in the first few chapters. Exploring the prospect of a quietist's refuge in nature is a continuation of the theme.

A further answer is that natural environments are the refuges that figure by far the most saliently in the literature of refuge. The rhetoric of refuge in nature is unparalleled by one of refuge in anything else. We've already encountered examples of it, for instance in Wordsworth's lament that we have become "out of tune" with nature. A few decades after Wordsworth's poem, Thoreau wrote of the "sweet and tender

...innocent and encouraging society" to be found in nature, even for a "poor misanthrope" like himself.[1] A century later, another American misanthrope, the environmentalist and anarchist, Edward Abbey, proposed that, since "the world of men is...ugly, cruel, trivial [and] unjust", the only thing for an "honest man" is to withdraw and "cultivate your own garden [or] look to the mountains".[2] Characters in a book by W. G. Sebald, tired of existence in the "so-called real world", resolve to spend their lives out of doors, with "plants and animals" as their "companions".[3]

The idea of nature as refuge is also pervasive in Asian quietist traditions. It is commonplace, for example, among the Tang poets. When Wang Wei becomes sick of "the affairs of the world", it is to his "old forest home" that he goes.[4] The Daoist monasteries to which poets often repaired were typically situated in remote natural environments. The idea is prominent, too, in the *Theragāthā*, the verses composed – with some later additions – by Buddhist monks during the Buddha's lifetime. Finding the human world "loathsome" and full of "discontent with th[at] world", the monks "go to the forest", sit on the banks of rivers, or stay in a "lonely grove". In such places, they find "delight", serenity, beauty, and the opportunity for "detachment".[5]

We should recognize, too, that some other places mentioned in Chapter 6 partly owe their aptness to provide refuge to their natural locations. For example, the Daoist monasteries just mentioned and the huts which many quietists have chosen to inhabit are, typically, set in natural environments. The several deeply pessimistic Japanese Buddhist monks and poets who found refuge in their huts testify to the importance of these environments. Chomei, early in the thirteenth century, escapes from the "torn world" of human affairs to live in a

10ft square hut where he is at peace in the woods, surrounded by the "friends" he finds in nature. A century after, the Zen monk, Shiwu ("Stonehouse"), "leaves the world behind" and finds contentment in a "well-hidden hut" surrounded by bamboo, rocks, gibbons and cranes.[6]

Relationship to nature has also been significant in the decisions of Western thinkers, disillusioned by the direction of modern civilization, to spend time in huts. Depressed by a world in which everything was increasingly perceived as mere "equipment" for human use, Martin Heidegger felt "at home" only in his mountain valley cabin, where he could experience "the powers of encompassing nature".[7] In his little cottage by the fields and woods near to his monastery, Thomas Merton did not feel "alien", in the way he felt "alien to the noise of cities, of people, to the greed of machinery".[8] Whether by Walden Pond, in a Black Forest valley, on a Norwegian fjord (where Wittgenstein had a cottage constructed), or the grounds of an abbey in Kentucky, huts have served as refuges because of their location in nature.

Merton found his monastery too noisy, but monasteries have themselves been significant places of refuge in many religious cultures. Visitors to monasteries – or their ruins – are impressed by how carefully their natural sites were chosen. A tour of ruined monasteries in the north of England – Holy Island, Rievaulx, Mount Grace, Fountains – takes one from the edge of the sea to sheltered valleys to the banks of wooded rivers. In Sri Lanka, Buddhists "take refuge" in the *sangha*, the community of monks, whose monasteries often perch on cliffs, peek out from the jungle, or stand on an island in a lake. It is easy to understand, visiting these places, how they offer refuge and promise a peace that, as the last prior of Mount Grace laconically put it, is "hard for worldly men" to experience.

A significant component of Christian and Buddhist monasteries alike is the garden. And the garden, of course, is another place that has invited the rhetoric of refuge.[9] The Japanese poet-monk, Ryōkan, sits among the trees in a friend's garden, enjoying its "separation from the world" and finding in this "tranquil place ... the spirit of Zen".[10] The twentieth-century Californian garden designer, Thomas Church, wanted to create a "green oasis" where his clients could forget work and their "bumper-to-bumper ride" home.[11] Gardens may be situated in or close to natural environments, and many of them are to a degree natural places. Although designed and maintained by human beings, gardens are places in which natural, organic processes of generation and death, growth and decay, decomposition, photosynthesis and so on are continually at work in it. The same is true of other so-called "hybrid" or "humanized" landscapes, such as parks.

Gardens, of course, are places people may spend time in for reasons besides that of refuge – to enjoy garden parties, to save money by growing vegetables, or simply to admire flowers and shrubs. The same is true of natural places generally. For some people, it seems, nature is something of an assault course, offering challenges to overcome – mountains to conquer, rapids to ride, trails to blaze. For others, nature is a killing field, the supplier of creatures that they can have fun shooting, hooking, trapping, or setting dogs upon. For yet others, to judge from the empty bottles and litter encountered on country walks, nature can be, as it were, an open-air nightclub.

These don't sound like the activities of a quietist, although such is the complexity of the human soul that it is not unknown for a person to combine, say, a love of hunting with a more serene appreciation of nature. The man who shoots a leopard in the afternoon may, in the evening, as he sits beneath the stars outside his tent, experience a sense of refuge from a human world he has come to despise. So, at least, writers like Ernest Hemingway try to convince us.

The important thing, however, in assessing whether a natural place is a refuge for someone is not *what* activities are engaged in. Rather, it is whether the place is regarded under the aspects of refuge described in Chapter 6 – as "another" and a "better place". Many people nowadays spend time in nature for reasons of health, both physical and mental. "Nature therapy" – "forest bathing" and "wild swimming", for instance – has become big business.[12] What those in search of the benefits of therapy *do* – walk, swim, climb, or just look – may be the same as what seekers of refuge do. But the motives and perceptions are not the same, even though the differences are not sharp. It might be hard, in practice, to distinguish the pessimistic disquiet that prompts a need for refuge from reasons, like a desire to get away from the stress of the workplace, that motivate someone to turn to nature therapy. In what follows it is upon nature as a refuge from disquiet that I focus.

"ANOTHER PLACE"

If the metaphor of natural places as refuges is to be compelling, there must be analogies with places where refugees, in the literal sense, seek refuge. A natural place must, crucially, be "another" place, significantly "other" than the world of human affairs. This other place is not a merely geographical location or entity. When we speak of people being in the mountains, rainforest, or garden, we don't usually or simply mean that this is where they are physically located. To "be in", in the relevant sense, is to be engaged in some way with a place – climbing, sight-seeing, digging, or whatever. The place is not a physical container but, to recall an earlier discussion, a theatre of significance, of engagement and of possibilities for experiences hard to find elsewhere.

What does it mean to say that a natural place, so understood, is "other" than the human world? Various typical differences are easily stated. Most of the living beings, whether flora or fauna, encountered in a natural environment are not human beings, and the stuffs or substances one comes across – seawater, soil, rock – are very different from those, like steel, plastic, and concrete that are ubiquitous in the human world. With the exception of certain "hybrid" landscapes – gnome-filled gardens, for instance, or sculpture parks – natural places do not typically contain any or many artefacts. And while it is possible to put natural environments to practical use – to treat them as resources or equipment – this is not why they are there, unlike power stations and supermarkets.

These obvious differences, however, do not guarantee the sense of otherness that a natural place must convey in order to serve as a refuge. The existence of these differences is, for some people, of no emotional significance. It wouldn't matter to their experience of a place whether, for example, the birds and trees the tourist guide takes them to see are real or artificial. Such people do not feel, in natural places, any sense of escape from the human world. Indeed, they may be anxious to get back to the city – in some cases, one suspects, because being in natural places threatens to prompt uncomfortable reflection on urban existence.

To identify less obvious aspects of nature's otherness, let's begin with the complaint of several authors that, when we describe nature, we are imposing our own ideas upon it, thereby occluding it or distorting how it really is. The novelist,

John Fowles, wrote that describing or conceptualizing a plant or animal is to insert "a pane of dirty glass between you and it".[13] Thomas Merton regards nature as we describe it as the "product" of our knowledge. Our "ideas of nature ... [are] all very well" for practical purposes, he writes, but nature itself is "*neti, neti*" ("not this, not that").[14] It is not only lovers of nature who make this point. Sartre, always uncomfortable outside of the city, disliked nature for its fluidity and opacity. The cause of Roquentin's discomfort or "nausea" at the sight of a chestnut root was its brute "thereness", its refusal to be captured by our words and concepts.[15]

There is something to this point, but it's hard to get it right. It's not true, for a start, that words and concepts don't genuinely apply to nature. What I now see outside my study window is a pigeon, a creature to which the word "pigeon" correctly refers, and the cause of Roquentin's nausea was what he himself rightly names a "chestnut root". Nor is it easy to fathom the vocabulary of "thereness", "suchness", "beingness" or "brute existence" to which authors resort when trying to characterize how nature "really" is, "in itself".

So, how might we make sense of the idea of nature as "another world"? Let's start in the kitchen. My kitchen is very much "my world", one in which nearly everything – coffee maker, plate rack, chopping board, Alexa – is geared to my needs. More generally, places in the everyday world of human affairs – offices, bus stations, supermarkets – are organized in relation to social and individual needs and purposes: they belong to "our world".

The terms and concepts we apply to things in our world – "coffee maker" and so on – apply to things in virtue of their utility or function. There's no question, here, of our "imposing" concepts on these things: the coffee maker demands to be called a coffee maker, for that is what it is, and anyone who doesn't recognize it as a coffee maker is ignorant of what it is. Because these are functional concepts, their application is generally precise. Something else might look rather like a coffee maker, but if that is not its function, it is a quite different object. There is little or no fuzziness in the term "coffee maker". The machine can't be *almost* or *more or less* a coffee maker, except perhaps in the sense that parts are missing or damaged.

An implication of these points is that creatures whose form of life is very different from ours – one largely free from technology, say – won't recognize most of what is in the kitchen, office or bus station. For these do not belong in their world, but in our world. These creatures are ignorant about the constituents of our world and would have to be educated in order to understand them. Compare this to the way in which people today need to be educated, in museums or by television documentaries, in order to understand and even identify items of Victorian engineering.

Now contrast this with natural places, for example the wooded, hilly and rocky headland that I am looking at across a loch. The terms I just used to describe it, like "hilly", are not functional ones: they don't apply to things in virtue of their utility. Hills are what they are independently of our needs and desires. Because they are not neatly defined in functional terms, "hill", "wood" and so on are fuzzy concepts. When does a hill become a mountain, a wood a forest, a bush a tree? Geologists and botanists may work with concepts of these things more precise than our everyday ones. But they are artificial – fine for certain taxonomic purposes, but with little relevance to ordinary experience of landscapes. They impose dividing lines where, for experience, there is only gradation.

These remarks entail that creatures who do not classify and conceptualize a natural place as we do cannot be accused of ignorance, of a failure of recognition. If we do so accuse them, they could accuse us in return. The headland, unlike a kitchen or office, is not divided up into functional objects that dictate which concepts to apply. Creatures unlike ourselves will group natural things together and distinguish between them very differently from us – and in ways that are neither better nor worse, more nor less accurate, than ours.

This difference between concepts – functional versus natural – has its parallel in perceptual or phenomenological differences. When I walk on the headland, the unfolding scene does not neatly divide itself up into objects that starkly stand out from everything else, demanding individual attention in the way the coffee maker does. I am free to focus on what aspects of the scene I choose – what expanse of woodland, what part of the hill, which scudding clouds. In contrast to artworks, moreover, nothing dictates the distance, angle or perspective from which I should admire the scene. No one could appreciate a painting from 10 centimetres or 100 metres away: but I can admire the tree, albeit in different ways, from either distance.[16] We can be certain that other creatures – birds, animals, our distant ancestors – experience natural places very differently from ourselves. Things will stand out for them, given their kinds of life, that do not do so for us – and vice-versa. It is certain, too, that they experience natural places without being lost or confused like the alien intruders in my kitchen or office. How "ridiculous", exclaimed Thoreau, to imagine that "Nature could only support but one order of understandings, could not sustain [that of] birds as well as quadrupeds", of "creeping things" as well as Englishmen.[17]

The "otherness" of nature, I suggest, is to be understood, in part, in the light of these contrasts – conceptual and experiential – between our relations to the human world and to natural places respectively. It is not simply that in natural environments we encounter creatures, things, processes and stuffs very different from those in the everyday human world. More interestingly, they are neither experienced nor understood with reference to our needs and purposes, to the structures of life in which components of the human world are embedded. What makes a world "ours" are the identities and organization of its components according to their utility and function for us. It follows, then, that natural environments belong in "another" world, one in which we can be present, move and look without seeing "ourselves reflected back … without seeing in it our own desires and ambitions".[18]

Earlier, I questioned the complaint that description and conceptualization of nature is either impossible (it's "not this, not that") or necessarily distorting (like a dirty pane of glass). I questioned, too, the related claim that nature is a sort of undifferentiated "suchness" on which we force words and concepts. That said, my recent remarks encourage a degree of sympathy for the spirit, at least, of these claims.

Unlike lines of latitude and longitude, that have no reality in nature, concepts like those of mountains and forests are not imposed or projected on the world. There really are mountains and forests. It is imperative, though, to recognize the relativity of these concepts to the perspectives, interests, physical characteristics, and cultural traditions of human beings. There is nothing privileged about any set of such concepts, and it would be invidious and parochial to dismiss the conceptual repertoire of creatures with very different perspectives, interests and so on. Pride in the superiority of our concepts, Nietzsche observed, is as baseless as a gnat's pride in the superiority of its perspective.[19] Nature is no more our world than it is the gnat's – or the seagull's, rabbit's or deer's – world. To suppose otherwise is indeed to impose a particular perspective on what, as Thoreau puts it, "transgresses" our own limits. And it would mark a failure to recognize what, a few lines earlier, he calls the "unfathomable" character of nature – its permanent openness to new perspectives, experiences and vocabularies.[20] It is this unfathomableness, perhaps, that is gestured at by terms like "suchness" and "brute existence".

A natural place, then, qualifies as "another" place, hence as one that a person seeking relief from disquiet and refuge from the world that occasions it might turn to. But as we know in the case of refugees in the literal sense, the refuge sought must be a "better" and not simply "another" place. Before enquiring, in the next chapter, into how nature might provide "better" places than the human world, I shall make some remarks on what, for many people, is an especially important kind of refuge in which nature is at work – the garden.

GARDENS AND NATURE

We've already encountered references to gardens as refuges, such as Ryōkan's "tranquil place ... separate from the world", and these could be multiplied at will. One garden historian is almost right when he observes that, having once been "a place for man to escape from the threats of nature", the garden has become "a refuge from men".[21] But only almost, since as we know from Buddhist monks, Epicurus, Tang poets and Christian monastics, gardens have always been, for some people, refuges from the human world as much as, or more than, the dangers of nature.

The garden as refuge is too venerable and well-subscribed a metaphor to ignore. The question is whether it is a refuge comparable to a natural place, like the headland across the loch. Does it have the appropriate kind of "otherness"? The main reason for supposing that it is not comparable to the headland is unconvincing. According to this reason, gardens are quite unlike natural environments, since they are the products of human design, manufacture, cultivation and maintenance. A garden, far from being a natural place, is an imposition onto a natural place, no less than a car park built on former moorland is.

One problem with this line of thought is that, if a place ceases to be natural because it bears a human imprint, then there are few natural environments left on the planet. Indeed, if one includes in that imprint the effects of anthropogenic climate change – and of micro-plastics and "forever" chemicals – then there would be virtually no natural landscapes left. Some authors, of course, accept this conclusion and proclaim that we are therefore witnessing "the end of nature", or living in a world "after nature". But in any usual senses of "natural" and "nature", there remain countless natural places in the world, and for many of us much of the time nature is all around us. As the nature writer Robert Macfarlane points out, in a small wood close to a city – or in my back garden – the process of nature or "wildness" is "continually at work ... an organic existence, vigorous and chaotic".[22]

It is not the absence of human footprints that, in the relevant sense, makes a place natural, but this "organic existence". Nature ends where this existence ends – in the office, the bus station, the apartment block. (Although even here there may be pockets of nature – a shrub-filled atrium, say, or a roof covered with grass and herbs.) To be sure, there are gardens and gardens, and in some of these the processes of nature are so rigorously controlled – the freedom of trees, hedges and flowers to grow naturally so curtailed – that talk of imposition upon nature is apposite. Schopenhauer nicely distinguishes between "French" gardens, that are "tokens of [nature's] slavery", and "English" ones, that allow "the will of nature" to prevail.[23] It would please him that the latter type of garden is these days commonly referred to as "natural".

Where "the will of nature" and "wildness" are visibly at work in a garden, it offers refuge in a way comparable to that of the headland on the far side of the loch. Although I have had a large hand in shaping my garden, the things in it do not owe their identity and organization solely to their functions, to their catering to my needs and desires. It is not how it serves my purposes that makes something a rose bush, a sycamore tree or an earthworm. Unlike my office or kitchen, the garden is hardly more "my world" than it is the world of the birds, mice and insects that live in it. The Daoist sage, Liezi, described the "birds and animals [who] regard me as one of themselves" as becoming more at home in his garden than in the forests or marshes they have left.[24] The garden has become as much theirs to experience, understand and enjoy as it was his. The bird's experience and understanding will of course be different from the gardener's, but it would be invidious to privilege one over the other.

It matters little whether one finally describes a garden where "the will of nature" is visibly at work as a natural environment, a "hybrid" environment, or simply as a place with significant affinities to natural places like headlands and heaths. The important thing is to recognize these affinities and their implication for the "otherness" of such gardens. It is the affinities that equip these gardens to be refuges from the everyday human world. When one enters through the garden gate, it is not only the gate and the walls that separate the garden from the outside world. One enters into a place – "another world" – where nature prevails, or is at any rate busily at work. That is also why it is a refuge for those seeking relief from disquiet.

8

Nature as refuge 2: "A better place"

INNOCENCE

A refugee escaping from one country to another hopes to find there a better place. One hope is that the new place will be more innocent – less guilty – of what is being fled from, such as corruption and oppression. Here is the first way, I propose, in which, analogously, nature provides the quietist with a better place than, and so the prospect of refuge from, the human world. If nature is a realm of innocence, then it promises relief from the disquiet that shadows the pessimistic, misanthropic vision of humankind.

Among writers who have turned to nature for solace and refuge, the trope of nature's innocence is familiar. Thoreau refers to "the indescribable innocence and beneficence of nature" and the "cheer" that each affords.[1] The garden in Andrew Marvell's "Thoughts in a Garden" is a place not only of "delicious solitude", but of "fair quiet" and its "sister", "innocence". For the philosopher and dramatist, Friedrich Schiller, natural beings "*are* what we *were*" – our "lost childhood", where we "unnatural" creatures might again experience "pure innocence".[2]

But how can we regard nature as innocent, given the scale of pain, terrible deaths and other kinds of suffering that innumerable creatures experience in the natural world? Isn't nature, in the words of one philosopher, a very "cruel mistress"?[3] The nature writer, Annie Dillard, observes that "it is rough out there ... gruesome ... grotesque ... a universal chomp".[4] One reason the Buddha regards rebirth as an animal as terrible is because the lives of countless animals are themselves terrible.

Reminders like these rightly challenge romantic, sentimental conceptions of the natural world as a kind of Eden whose only blemish was Adam and Eve. Encouraged by poetry and paintings that represent nature as an idyll, by children's books full of cute creatures, by eco-tourist hype, and by dithyrambic television documentaries of the "What a Wonderful World" genre, such conceptions, although relatively recent, are remarkably popular and resilient. But they cannot, of course, be taken seriously. Reminders of the "universal chomp" also call into question the idea, promoted by "deep" ecologists, of nature as possessing "intrinsic" value. Only people indifferent to the pain and suffering of animals could be comfortable with that sort of language.

When I refer to nature as innocent, I do not, therefore, want to downplay the scale of suffering in nature – no more than, in speaking of the innocence of childhood, I want to deny that many children experience great pain. By the innocence of nature, I mean the absence of the vices and failings that, in Chapter 1, invited a negative verdict on the moral condition of humankind. Nature may indeed be a "cruel mistress", but not in any morally charged sense of "cruel" – a point endorsed by the same author when he denies that there is "wickedness" in the natural world, and describes it as "ethically neutral".[5]

With the possible, and debatable, exception of our relatively recent ancestors, the apes, animals are not cruel, deceptive, treacherous, self-obsessed, greedy, or heartless – not, that is, in senses of these terms that carry moral condemnation. Quite generally, animals are incapable of the understanding and intentions necessary for them to be guilty of moral failings.

The reason they are incapable was given, in effect, in Chapter 1, where I described the Buddha's diagnosis of humankind's moral condition. A precondition of our having moral failings is a sense of ourselves as relatively enduring selves or persons, whose lives stretch back into the past and forward into the future. Without such a sense, creatures cannot pursue long-term goals, nor manifest greed and ambition so as to achieve them. It is a sense necessary, too, if creatures are to become self-deceptive, self-absorbed and self-obsessed. Necessary, as well, if they are to measure themselves against each other and become susceptible to jealousy, envy and vanity. It is presupposed, finally, by the anxieties people experience with regard to their futures, their status and their worth – anxieties that drive people to maintain their security and self-esteem through aggression, bombast and self-delusion.

It is not exactly wrong to describe an animal's behaviour as, say, greedy or cruel, but these terms are then being used without their usual moral charge. Even inanimate things can be described with such terms, like greedy slot-machines or cruel winters. Greed, as a moral failing, is not ravenously stuffing down some food, but an inordinate desire to secure, for one's future benefit, greater wealth, sexual success, status and the like. A ravenous wolf cannot be greedy in this sense. Nor can it be cruel, in the morally charged sense of inflicting pain for reasons, like enjoyment or curiosity, other than the good of the creature being hurt. As Konrad Lorenz said of that voracious predator, the water shrew, it is only "innocently-cruel", unlike the man who "hunts for pleasure and not for food".[6]

So is nature "ethically neutral"? Not quite, since while animals are incapable of vice it does not follow that they are incapable of virtue. Arguably, there is an important asymmetry between vice and virtue.[7] While vice requires the capacities for understanding and intention just discussed, virtue may not. We can discern virtues – compassion, loyalty, sensitivity, gratitude – in the simple, unreflective behaviour of animals: in, for instance, the care exhibited by an elephant for her wounded sister. Not all virtues are unreflective, but some are. These take the form, in effect, of acting in keeping with simple, spontaneous moral emotions, some of which at least some kinds of animals manifest.

This asymmetry, however, is not a point I'll press here. It's enough, in order to establish the innocence of nature, to show that it is free from the vices and failings that are entrenched in human life. This innocence makes the natural world a better place. And it is an innocence, I want to say, that is palpable, one that we may experience, especially when we turn to nature for respite from daily and depressing encounters with human failings.

To confirm this, here's an experiment that people in a position to might try. Watch the early evening television news – with its customary litany of crime, violence, oppression, scandals and disasters, much of it reported on in prurient, intrusive or sanctimonious ways. Then switch it off, and go for some fresh air in the local wood or simply in one's garden. Listen to the blackbird's final song of the day, smell the resin from the pines, feel the cool breeze on one's face. Then, in and through these sensations, feel the innocence and clean-liness of the place, its distance from the human world and the absence from it of everything that stains people's lives in that world.

It is very likely that one will find the wood or the garden beautiful, for the beauty that we find in nature is, I suggest, not unrelated to its innocence. Nature's beauty is, of course, an aspect of it that helps to make it a better place. Kant writes that it is the beauty of nature that makes us "pleased at its [nature's] existence", in a way that the beauty of art does not necessarily make us pleased at the existence of the human world in which it is an ingredient.[8] The beauty of certain works of art will not overturn the verdict of those for whom it would have been better for humankind never to have evolved.

The "superiority which natural beauty has over that of art", continues Kant, is not due to presenting us with lovelier "forms", but to kinds of freedom it enjoys, like that of release from "the constraint of arbitrary rules". More generally, the beauty we admire in nature enjoys a freedom from embroil-ment with human affairs. This is freedom not only from rules and conventions, but from "minister[ing] to vanity or ... social joys", fashions and fads, snobbery, effeteness, financial interests, political ideologies, "woke" agendas, and everything else that might influence and corrupt the appreciation of beauty.[9]

It is the experience of the innocence of nature that helps to resolve a puzzle that Kant rightly notes. Why is it that the beauty I experience "vanishes completely" when I learn that I've been duped – that, say, the trees I've been admiring are clever fakes, or that the birdsong I was enjoying is elec-tronically produced? After all, the look or sound itself hasn't altered. Kant's solution is that, on discovering the deceit, the "*feeling* for beautiful nature" evaporates, for we are returned to the human world of artifacts, ingenuity, profit and fashion.[10] We are jolted from the realm of innocence back to the world of human involvements. This jolt prompts recognition not only of nature's innocence, but of this innocence as a reason for enjoyment of natural places and so for going to them for refuge.

VIRTUES

A second reason why the natural world is a "better place" is that it is an arena in which to cultivate and exercise virtues that are harder to acquire or maintain in the course of human affairs. Indeed, they are virtues often marginalized or disparaged in everyday life. Nature is a place, therefore, apt for the exercise of the "humaneness" that, as we saw in Chapter 5, supplements the quietist's strategy of detachment and disengagement.

Like the innocence of nature, the idea of nature as a moral arena is well-attested to. Zhuangzi, for example, puts into the mouth of the legendary Yellow Emperor, who finds himself playing his zither in "the wilds of Dongting", among insects and birds, a declaration of "perfect joy". This joy is due, not least, to his manifesting "the Five Virtues" (including kindness and moderation), adherence to "the Heavenly", fluid spontaneity, and a sense of bringing harmony to "the ten thousand things".[11] In the *Theragāthā*, several of the Buddhist monks speak of the virtues that, in the peace of natural places – forests, rivers, meadows – they are able to nurture, including compassion, resoluteness and equanimity. More generally, in such environments they are capable of "annihilating the cankers" of existence in a "depraved" and "loathsome" world. For Schiller, those with a developed sensitivity to nature – to flowers, bees, brooks, birds – experience "a kind of love and tender respect", and a moral regard for it that is not easily replicated in our "degenerate" and "depraved" social life.[12]

One of the Buddhist Elders remarked that, if we could "see the world as being like grass and wood", we would see that the world is "not mine".[13] The theme is picked up two millennia later by Iris Murdoch, who illustrates "unselfing" with her experience of a hovering kestrel that so absorbs her attention that her "brooding self" – with its "hurt vanity" and anxiety about prestige – disappears.[14] "Unselfing", for Murdoch – as for the Buddha – is a precondition of living well and virtuously, and it is striking that she, like the Elders, chooses an experience of nature to exemplify it. Striking, but not unfamiliar. Rousseau, for instance, recounts how he "forgets himself" as he rambles through woods and fields.[15]

But why should natural environments be especially apt for "unselfing" and the exercise of virtues? Much of the answer is contained in Murdoch's reference to the "self-forgetful pleasure we take in the sheer alien pointless independent existence of animals, birds, stones and trees".[16] What those four adjectives before "existence" indicate is what I've been calling the "otherness" and "innocence" of nature. Nature is, unless we commandeer it, not defined in relation to human purposes, not identified through its functions, and is without the failings that mark the human condition.

When we experience nature for what it is, then engagement with it will display that "selfless respect for reality" that Murdoch calls "humility". And with this respect comes a readiness to care and protect, to treat things with equanimity and impartiality. For when nature is perceived as standing outside the world of purposes, ambitions, self-interest, prejudices and jealousies, there is nothing in it to invite cruelty, aggression, bad faith and our other many failings. (This may be why people especially embroiled in and conditioned to that world find natural environments boring.) Indeed, animals, flowers and so on, in their "otherness" and innocence, are liable to give pleasure through, as Schiller put it, "being models for us", through displaying "exactly what [we] lack ... to be perfect".[17] It is, wrote Kierkegaard, the lily of the field and the bird of the air that we should regard as "teachers", from whom to learn the virtues of humility and obedience, love and joy.[18]

It is important to emphasize that the quiet virtues whose exercise is invited in the presence of nature – humility, spontaneity, care, reticence, patience, attentiveness and so on – are those least encouraged and admired in modern everyday life. On the contrary, people are instead exhorted to be "assertive" and "passionate", to "make a difference" and "protest" loudly, not to "waste time", and to "achieve". Over two thousand years ago, Daoist poets and Buddhist monks were certain that they needed to go to the forests, hills and rivers properly to cultivate these quiet virtues. Their certainty would be even stronger were they around today.

Earlier, I suggested that the enjoyment of natural beauty was intimately related to a sense of nature's innocence. There are similar close connections between this beauty and the idea of nature as an arena for exercising virtues. If by "virtue" is meant what contributes to living well – to a good life – then the appreciation of beauty is itself a virtue. Confucius and Plato, to name just two, would endorse this claim. But let's waive the question of whether enjoyment of beauty is itself a virtue. Surely it is at any rate what Iris Murdoch calls it – "patently a good thing".[19]

What makes it a "good thing" is not just the pleasure and joy that beauty brings, but its role in making the exercise of the virtues attractive. This role is apparent in many small, but significant ways. In Japan, for instance, skill goes into ensuring that the devices used to protect trees from heavy snow do not detract from the beauty of the trees. Otherwise people might be less inclined to care for the trees.[20] It is the beauty I find in the birds that visit my garden – including "little brown things" – that helps to ensure that I shall be solicitous about their well-being in the coming winter. In the *Theragāthā*, it is the joy that the monks experience at the beauty of rocks, peacocks, crags, flowers and birds that inspires in them a wish to be compassionate, mindful and resolute.

As much as anything, it was the ugliness of the landscape degraded by logging and fish-farming that depressed the man in my Prologue about humankind's treatment of the natural world. An example like this implies that it can be difficult, even pointless, to keep separate one's aesthetic experience from one's moral understanding. Just as learning that the trees were fake erased the enjoyment of looking at them, so being informed that a moorland is a killing-ground for recreational hunters can destroy the pleasure of viewing it.

It is not easy to explain such cases unless one agrees with Kant that the interest we have in the beauty of nature is "akin to the moral". The person blind to this beauty is "coarse and low", whereas openness to it is a mark of a "good", indeed "beautiful soul".[21] These remarks could be taken to mean only that moral understanding affects our appreciation of natural beauty while, in turn, this appreciation inflects and reinforces moral perceptions. So taken, the remarks simply indicate the role beauty plays in regarding nature as an arena for the exercise of virtues. I say "only" and "simply", not because this is in any way an insignificant or obvious point, but because Kant himself has something rather more opaque in mind, a deeper point about an authentic relationship with nature. We *ought* to enjoy natural beauty, he writes, not only because this contributes to certain virtues, but because it points to an "idea" of nature – to nature as a "ground" – that should inform the moral life.[22] This thought is one I return to shortly.

FREEDOM AND BELONGING

Refugees may be fleeing political or religious oppression, looking to enjoy in a new location freedoms denied them at home. Likewise, the quietist seeks a place of refuge where freedoms may be found that are difficult or impossible to exercise in the everyday human world. It will be a place where, for a time at least, the quietist is released from the context of ambitions, pressures on achievement, jealousies, busyness, and everything else that drew the pessimistic, misanthropic verdict on the human world. The quietist aspiration, like the Buddha's, is liberation from "the worldly conditions", from what brings disquiet and suffering.

Nature, many writers testify, provides places of freedom. The Chinese poet, Tao Yuanming, describes how, when he is able to get away from his work in the city and "return to nature", he is no longer "trapped in a cage" and "the world's dusty net".[23] In his essay, "Walking", Thoreau "wish[es] to speak a word for Nature, for absolute freedom . . . , as contrasted with a freedom . . . merely civil".[24] Other enthusiastic walkers agree. Zhuangzi, for instance, finds that "the heart-mind wanders freely" when "rambling", while the haiku poet, Bashō, observes that his journeys on foot are restricted by "no rules". Rousseau, too, in his *Reveries of a Solitary Walker*, records how, as he rambles through the countryside, his ideas "follow their own bent without constraint".[25]

It is no surprise, of course, that being in natural places invites experiences of freedom. Nature, we've seen, is "another place" – one where rules, commitments, the pursuits of success and prestige and much else that constrain people in the human world hold no sway. The human world, said Sartre, is "a world of tasks":[26] the natural world isn't. This is why many people go to natural places for therapeutic purposes, to "de-stress", or to "recharge batteries". The quietist looks for something more abiding and more informed by a perception of the human condition than therapy, but, as noted earlier, there is no sharp line between relief from disquiet and therapeutic goals.

Important for several writers is nature's provision of symbols of freedom. "Free!", exclaimed J. A. Baker, "you cannot know what freedom means till you have seen a peregrine loosed into the warm spring sky".[27] For Zhuangzi, even fish are symbolic of freedom: "the minnows swim about so freely", smoothly darting past one another and avoiding confrontation.[28] "Symbol" here has the sense it had for Romantic authors: unlike a mere sign, a symbol is taken, rightly or not, saliently to embody or exemplify what it stands for. Lions are therefore symbols of strength and, for the writers just cited, birds and fish are symbols of freedom.

One reason for attending to natural symbols is that, as salient exemplars of freedom, they also make salient a contrasting lack of freedom in the human world. For Baker, the freedom that we "smug" human beings boast of is a poor substitute for the falcon's. A main theme of Zhuangzi's is that, in contrast with the lives of fish, those of human beings who have "lost the Way" – most of us, that is – are awkward, fractious, rigid and confrontational. Recognition of these contrasts then becomes a reason to emulate natural freedom in one's own life. Its freedom, wrote the "inhumanist" poet, Robinson Jeffers, is one reason to "labour to be like" nature.[29] Freeing up our capacity for sensory enjoyment of the world is also a reason for "becoming animal", to cite the title of a book by the environmental thinker, David Abram.

For some, it is not this or that particular animal or plant so much as nature as a whole that embodies and symbolizes freedom. This is part, at least, of what Kant meant by an "idea" of nature that informs the moral life. In nature, his admirer Schiller wrote, we discern "the silent creativity" and "free power" of life.[30] But it is in the Daoist classics that the idea is, perhaps, most developed. The freedom in question is that of "spontaneity" (*ziran*), for the processes of nature are the unfolding of the *dao* that itself "follows the way of spontaneity".[31] Nature contends with nothing, is governed by nothing outside it, and does not impose or force itself on anything.

Nature, in this vision, is – to anticipate a theme of Chapter 9 – a giant model of how we should live, a place whose palpable spirit of spontaneity should inspire our existence. Alone among creatures, human beings can "lose the Way" and act in opposition to what is natural. The Daoist imperative to is to regain a lost spontaneity – to live, in effect, in the style of *wu wei* ("not doing"). "Not doing" was, of course, a significant component of the quietist mode of life discussed in Chapter 5 – a mode of detachment, equanimity and humility. The spontaneity of "not doing" is not caprice or whim, but "responsiveness in the impersonal calm when vision is most lucid".[32] This remark, from a commentator on Daoism, might easily have occurred in Baker's description of the freedom that the peregrine symbolizes.

A creature whose vision of its environment is lucid, untroubled, objective and appropriately responsive to what occurs there, is one that understands the environment. Animals that understand their environments *belong* in them, are "at home" in them. So we are led to another trope – that of natural places as ones to which human beings may and should belong. "[O]ver-civilised people are beginning to find out", wrote the great champion of National Parks in the USA, John Muir, "that going to the mountains is going home".[33] Thoreau wished not only to "speak a word for Nature" and freedom, but to "regard man as an inhabitant, or a part and parcel of Nature".[34]

It would be a mistake to think that claims like these contradict the conception of nature as "another place" from the human world. The point of that expression was not that nature must feel alien and uncanny to human beings – we modern ones, at any rate – but that it enjoys a certain independence. There is no inconsistency, for example, on the part of the character in one of Karl Ove Knausgaard's novels who is "struck with force" by how "*other*" a landscape and seascape are, but also wants "the place to inhabit me, and I it".[35] Not only are natural places relatively free from human imposition and control, but they can be understood and experienced without reference to human needs and purposes. Nature, to recall Thoreau's words, is recognized as having an "unfathomable" aspect that "transgresses" the limits of our understanding and perception of the human world.

Claims like Muir's and Thoreau's are sometimes associated with the idea of "biophilia", according to which, as creatures evolved from ancestors whose homes were in wild places, we are innately prone to feel a close affinity with nature.[36] This feeling, however, has largely been suppressed, so it's argued, with the development of agriculture, industry and urbanization. There may be something to this speculation, but it is not necessary for explaining a sense of belonging in nature. It is enough to give reminders of the ways in which those who turn to natural places for refuge become familiar with them, know their way about, respond to them, and are at ease there.

The understanding of places here is not the theoretical kind displayed by the botanist or zoologist – a kind that might in fact be an obstacle to this understanding. It is an understanding that, as phenomenologists like to say, is "in the hands" rather than "in the head" – the kind displayed by the skilled practitioners who figure in Daoist texts. It is the practical know-how of the swimmer when going with the current of the river, the hiker when gauging the steepness of an incline, or the bird-watcher when anticipating the falcon's next move. To have a sense of belonging in such places is to experience them as, so to speak, theatres of meaning, in which the significance of things – the incline, the current, the flap of a wing – is recognized and responded to. In this respect, a natural place in which one belongs is like a language or a piece of music with which one is familiar.

But don't we also belong in – feel at ease in, know our way around, understand – plenty of places in the everyday human world? In our homes, offices, colleges, clubs and so on? If so, what is special about natural places? It is true, of course, that a person may feel at home in many human environments, though it is worth stressing that there will also be many that, although very familiar, invite no sense of belonging. One just doesn't know how to deal with one's awkward, perhaps hostile, colleagues, say. But there is a precarious fragility in one's relationship to human environments that is missing in the case of natural ones.

This is due, in part, to the unreliability of one's fellows. An unfaithful partner, a jealous employer, an infatuated student, or a corrupt club secretary can turn a place where a person felt at home into an alien environment, fraught with anxiety and uncertainty. Natural places, too, have their dangers – the concealed viper, the thin ice, the looming storm – but these are budgeted for by the experienced rambler, climber, or gardener. They do not contribute to a general anxiety to which human beings are prone in their dealings with one another. This is because natural places, being "other", are not totally embroiled in a context of ambitions, desires, purposes, worries about status, and so on. And this is also why natural hazards do not reflect badly on nature, whereas the traps and threats we face in the human world are further evidence of our vices and failings.

In the eighth of his *Duino Elegies*, the German poet, Rainer Maria Rilke, unfavourably contrasts human with animal lives. Unlike animals, we are "turned *in* on everything", unhealthily focused upon our own selves and interests. And because we are obsessively in pursuit of goals and future achievements, we constantly give the impression of "someone just about to depart".[37] Never living entirely in the present, we are always, as Rilke's admirer, Heidegger, put it, "ahead of ourselves" and "on the way" to future accomplishments or failures.[38] The homes – the places of belonging – that we find in the human world are, in Rilke's words, "windy and precarious".

Human beings are not, of course, in natural places in the same way the animals who live there are. Fully "becoming animal" is not an option for enculturated and civilized creatures participating in human forms of life. But nature

117

provides people with refuge, in part, through enabling a way of belonging in natural places that is not disjoined from that of animals. It is a way, at least, that is less precarious and replete with anxiety than the ways found in the world of human affairs. And here, in this kind of belonging, is one more reason – in addition to its innocence and scope for exercising freedom and the virtues – why nature is "a better place", and hence a place of refuge.

9

Quietism, truth and mystery

TAKING STOCK

This is a short book, but it has covered a lot of ground. It will be helpful briefly to go over some of this ground in order to provide a setting for the reflections in this final chapter.

In the Prologue, a disturbing experience of environmental devastation – though it could as well have been one of "man's inhumanity to man" – prompted a dark perception of the human condition. This perception helped to endorse the judgements on the human condition, discussed in Chapter 1, that are made by pessimists and misanthropists. The state of humankind as it has developed is, the pessimist recognizes, saturated by suffering, anxiety, unsatisfied desires or satiated boredom, fear of death, and much else that makes human life "unsatisfactory". Nor is it realistic to expect any radical change in this condition. The negative assessment is compounded by a misanthropic judgement on the human condition as marked by deep, general and entrenched failings and vices. Indeed, that's one reason why no radical melioration of our condition can be envisaged. Pessimism and misanthropy, as we saw, typically reinforce one another.

Pessimism and misanthropy are judgements on the human condition, not mere feelings, but if they are judgements that are genuinely embraced or endorsed, they must be accompanied by a negative mood. I named this "disquiet" – a term that can cover more particular moods like despair, disgust and anxiety. The question addressed in the chapters following was how a person should live in the light of the pessimistic, misanthropic verdict. How should a person accommodate disquiet? This, it was emphasized, is indeed a personal question. The issue is not how "We" – human beings at large, "society" – should respond to pessimism and misanthropy. No such response – a global moral revolution, say – will occur, and that it won't is part of the context in which an individual person should reflect on how to live.

After rejecting various responses to pessimism, misanthropy and disquiet – including, especially, "activist" attempts to improve the human condition – I defended what I labelled "quietism". Borrowing from Daoist and Confucian concepts, this was characterized as "humane *wu wei*" (not doing). The quietist's life aspires to be flexible and spontaneous, disentangled from the busyness of the world, uncontending, distanced from rigid rules, conventions, dogmas and prejudice, compassionate, modest in its moral ambitions, and displaying appreciation of beauty. Humane "not doers", I proposed, are close to realizing quietist aspirations of tranquillity, equanimity, freedom from a range of human failings, and clear understanding.

In Chapter 6, however, I argued that "humane not doing" is an insufficiently "positive" goal for quietists in search of relief from disquiet. They require, as well, "refuge" from the everyday world of human failings and discontent – "another" and "better" place into which to retreat. The following chapters explored the idea of nature – of natural environments – providing such a refuge. Nature is "other" in that our experience of it does not have to be – and should not be – dictated, in the way experience of the human world is, by functional, utilitarian purposes. It is a "better" place, not only through being a realm of "innocence", but by providing an arena hospitable to the cultivation of certain virtues, as well as to senses of freedom and belonging.

That's where we've reached. The question now is whether we've reached the end. Does quietism, supplemented with the finding of refuge in nature (or some other "place"), constitute a sufficient response to a negative verdict on the human condition and the disquiet this entails? Some will answer "No" to these questions, urging that something is still missing from the quietist response. What is at issue here is deep and murky, and calls for a more extended treatment than I have space for. But it would be wrong to close the book without raising it and inviting readers to reflect upon it.

TRUTH, REALITY AND NATURE

There are two, converging, ways to appreciate the extra dimension that, some will argue, is required for a complete accommodation with disquiet. The first recalls a theme we've heard occasionally, but which has remained recessive – that of living, to recall Kierkegaard's expression, "in the truth". It's time, in effect, to resurrect the worry, briefly raised at the end of Chapter 5, that quietists have not so far addressed this theme.

Among the human failings identified by the misanthropist, several are at once moral and epistemic: culpable ignorance, wishful thinking, prejudiced opinion, readiness to accept dogmas and ideologies, and so on. A quietist aspiration, accordingly, is to minimize such failings in one's life. Arguably, however, something more ambitious is required than reduction of these epistemic vices. This is the attempt to make one's life consonant with a right understanding of the way of things, of how reality is. Without a sense of consonance, it'll be said, a person is open to the anxiety that quietism and refuge are, as it were, an indulgence – personally satisfying, perhaps, but without any grounding in the way of things. Put differently, the fear will remain – a fear potentially destructive of the tranquillity quietists seek – that the quietist life is not "in the truth". If, for example, a theistic conception of reality is right, then a quietist life that does not conform to this vision fails to be "in the truth".

A second reason for adding a further dimension to the quietist strategy for an accommodation with disquiet has to do with the refuge in nature that became part of this strategy. Earlier, I cited several authors of a quietist disposition who regard nature as a refuge. What I've barely cited are testimonies, by these and other writers, to what they regard as an essential aspect of experience of nature. Here is a famous example of the relevant kind of testimony. In some much-quoted lines of his poem written above Tintern Abbey, overlooking the Wye Valley, Wordsworth records "his sense sublime of something far more deeply interfused ... A motion and a spirit that impels ... and rolls through all things".[1]

What Wordsworth's lines register is an experience of natural places that is also "a disclosure of how the world really is".[2] There are experiences of nature that engender a sense of the fundamental way of things. *What* is intimated is a matter on which writers differ, as we'll see. But, first, let's simply note how this theme of the significance of experiences of nature converges with that of being "in the truth". Wordsworth's vision is one of how reality is. If it is a true vision, then it is one which a person's life should be consonant with and informed by for this life to be led "in the truth".

At least three variants of the theme are worth indicating. One is the theistic idea that in observing the wonders of nature, a person is experiencing the presence of God. Kierkegaard was a great lover of nature, not least because of the "unseen" realm it pointed to. Recalling the medieval image of nature as "The Book of God", he writes of rainbows and other "signs by which God's greatness in nature is known".[3] The twentieth-century Greek Orthodox poet and essayist, Zissimos Lorenzatos, speaks of "a sense of returning to the world of God", and of "separation from the world of man", occasioned by his experience of the ocean, the earth and the firmament.[4]

Second are testimonies to a more pantheistic vision inspired by experiences of nature. ("Panentheism" – the idea that the world is somehow included in, but not identical with, the divine – might be the better term.) This, perhaps, is how Wordsworth's "spirit" that "rolls through all things" is to be construed. Thoreau speaks of nature as a "vast and universal ... personality", accessible to those genuinely open to nature's beauty.[5] Wordsworth's friend Coleridge's God is one who is "in all things", just as "all things [are] in Himself", identical perhaps with what the poet elsewhere calls "the One Life within us and abroad / Which meets all motion and becomes its soul".[6] A modern defender of panentheism describes nature as the "power" of "the Highest One", an "outpouring of Being".[7]

Finally, there are the many testimonies that, without personifying and drawing on theological concepts, attest to

123

experiences of natural phenomena that furnish a sense of a "power" or "energy" that courses through everything. Gustav Mahler, explaining the aims of his Third Symphony, refers to "nature's mystic power" that "science can[not] reach".[8] His French contemporary, Henri Bergson, was also writing of a "vital impetus" (*élan vital*), a "great river of life", that shapes everything that happens and which "mystical experience" – free from the "static", analytical style of scientific observation – enables us to discern in nature.[9]

The general idea of a "power" that is ultimately responsible for what and how things are in the world, and which can be experienced by the enlightened person, is familiar, too, of course in several Asian traditions. The Chinese concepts of *qi* and *dao*, and the Vedic notion of *rta*, are not identical, but each is as an impersonal, active and animating power or force without which nothing would be brought into being and nothing would be what it is.[10] The *dao*, for example, is said to "run through and connect everything", and to be responsible for the existence of "the myriad things".[11]

While it is useful to distinguish different forms of the idea that experience of nature discloses "how the world really is", the distinctions should not be taken as sharp. It's often unclear to which form a particular claim should be allocated. I took Wordsworth's mention of a "spirit" that rolls through all things to indicate a panentheistic orientation. But, perhaps the term was not intended to convey more than a power or force that drives all things, in which case Wordsworth's view might better align with that of Daoists, say, or Bergson.

It is unsurprising that the boundaries between variants of the general theme are uncertain, for proponents of nearly all the views I sketched agree that the words they employ are being used figuratively. "One life", "universal personality", "vital impetus" and so on at best gesture towards the reality that experience of nature discloses. What the opening of the *Daodejing* famously tells us of the *dao* – that it "cannot be spoken of", in literal terms at least – could equally be said of the other candidates.[12] Even the God to which he refers, Kierkegaard warns, can only be spoken of in language that, to avoid misunderstanding, we have constantly to "revoke".[13]

It is unsurprising, too, therefore, that terms like "mystery", "secret" and "mystical" enter the vocabulary that is reached for to characterize reality. Ronald Hepburn, a careful advocate of natural beauty as the disclosure of a "transcendent source for which we lack words and clear concepts", judged the label "nature-mysticism" to be appropriate for the views cited over the last few paragraphs.[14]

FROM QUIETISM TO TRUTH

It would take more space than I intend to devote to discuss in detail the various forms taken by the claim that experience of nature discloses the way of things. And even more space to attempt to adjudicate between them. But avoidance of these tasks does not entirely prevent addressing the question that concerns us. How, if at all, should a quietist's appreciation of the way of things, intimated by experiences of nature, affect the quietist response to pessimism, misanthropy and disquiet? How might the quietist's aspiration to live "in the truth" be realized by such an appreciation of how the world really is?

These are questions that quietists who have found refuge in nature take seriously. For them, to live in consonance with an understanding of the way of things completes an authentic response to disquiet. Humaneness, "not doing", tranquillity, refuge in nature – these and other components of the quietist life must have this consonance if that life is to be "in the truth". Such consonance provides, as it were, the consummation of quietism. So, for instance, only the person who "has the *dao*" – whose practice accords with, indeed emulates, the Way – achieves sagehood.[15] Only this person enjoys an authentic sense of being "in the truth" of things.

The styles of life deemed consonant will vary, of course, according to the particular account of reality in question. "Nature", wrote Mahler, "for us is the model"[16] – but what it is a model of or for varies among different thinkers. Kierkegaard urges us to "die to the world" and become "nothing before God" on seeing through nature to the "unseen" world beyond.[17] In contrast, the Daoist rhetoric is of a non-contending, spontaneous form of practice that manifests a vision of the *dao* evoked, say, by experience of flowing water.

Despite such metaphysical differences, there is considerable convergence, among the different views, on the kind of life that is "in the truth". This is due to their agreement that experience of nature points to a reality "for which we lack words and clear concepts". The exact character of Wordsworth's rolling "spirit", the *dao*, Coleridge's "One Life", Thoreau's "universal personality", and the rest must largely remain, like Tolstoy's God, "a secret of eternity" and "inevitably inexplicable".[18] Whether or not one speaks, in connection with these ideas, of "nature-mysticism", each acknowledges mystery in the way of things and invites us to be open to a sense of this mystery.

But how can this acknowledgement secure for quietists confidence that they are living "in the truth"? It might seem, after all, that by making a mystery of the way of things, nothing can be said or found that would provide a guide to living. This worry, however, ignores the possibility that attention to the very *sense* of the mystery of things confirms that the quietist way of life is "in the truth".

There are two aspects to this. The first is that quietist tranquillity, detachment and "not doing", as well as the exercise of quietist virtues and a quietist engagement with nature, are prerequisites for developing this sense. If a sense of mystery is "in the truth", then so is the kind of life that cultivates this sense. Second, a sense of mystery in turn encourages and fosters various quietist virtues and attitudes. The form of living conducive to a sense of mystery is thereby legitimated, as it were, by the very sense it has helped to cultivate.

However natural to our distant ancestors a sense of the mystery of things might have been, it has been marginalized, obstructed or derided in most modern cultures. We do not have to look far for factors that militate against it: for they are among the failings identified by the pessimist and the misanthropist in their assessment of the human condition. Human societies, as we've seen, are now characterized by a busyness, turbulence, hyperactivity, and thirst for achievement and accumulation that, as Zhuangzi put it, turn us into "galloping horses", unable to stop and take stock, exhausting ourselves and incapable of proper rest.[19] It hardly needs pointing out how inimical this tenor of life is to the calm and detachment recognized by the ancients as necessary to an appreciation of the way of things. As a later writer, Tolstoy, wrote, what is required for "receiving the truth" is not "especial active qualities of the mind", but "passive" ones like "renunciation of vanities" and "recognition of our material insignificance".[20]

Those last words might remind us of the forms of hubris that, in modernity, contribute to derision or occlusion of a sense of mystery. A supremely self-confident scientism will pronounce any such idea to be "spooky", to be dabbling in the "supernatural" or "occult". Then there is the perception of the natural world as a giant energy store, on tap for human use and benefit – a perception, compounded by a narrowly scientific conception of what reality is that leaves no space for a different vision of nature. There's the kind of hubris, too, encouraged, as we noted in Chapter 3, by today's activist ambitions and imperatives. A life of aggressive commitment, passion, protest, and righteous anger scarcely favours the tranquillity and equanimity traditionally seen as essential to a recognition of mystery. "Passion", the *Dhammapada* tells us, is "the ruin of people", the enemy of the "restrained, composed and contented" and of "peace".[21]

Someone will say that this sounds like a plea – one which few people these days are in a position to heed – to switch lanes from the *via activa* to the *via contemplativa*. Well, this would anyway be no objection to my or your making an attempt to switch: the fact that relatively few other people will be doing the same is neither here nor there. But, more importantly, it is wrong to suppose that cultivation of a sense of mystery must be through "contemplation", if this is understood solely or mainly in terms of mental concentration or meditation. It is a sense that may take shape through ordinary practices and engagements with nature.[22] The Daoist figures who recognize themselves to be "in the Way" include swimmers, craftsmen and butchers, whose awareness of the *dao* emerges in and through their practice. So if there is a plea for the *via contemplativa*, this is not for anything disjoined from engagement with things. The "not doing" that characterizes the quietist life is not, as Zhuangzi explained, doing nothing.

FROM TRUTH TO QUIETISM

If the quietist way is "in the truth" through being conducive to a sense of mystery, so it is through being encouraged by that very sense. More exactly, exercise of the "quiet" virtues is invited and induced by the recognition of mystery. It is important to emphasize here that recognition is not simply or mainly propositional knowledge, of the kind that a student might pick up from a philosophy text. It was a *sense* sublime, not some bit of information he was given, through which Wordsworth was aware of the spirit that rolls through all things. Sense, sensibility, attunement, feeling, mood … it is these relatively abiding and recurrent states through which the world presents itself as a mystery. It is these, with their affective charge, rather than theoretical knowledge, that invite and shape a living response.

Several of the quietist virtues invited can be placed under the rubric of "humility", one whose several shades we have encountered earlier. Fairly obviously, a sense of mystery invites intellectual humility, a recognition that the limits to human knowledge of reality are not temporary, contingent ones that further research will remove. Humility, here, is an appreciation that, to cite Tolstoy once more, "everything inexplicable presents itself as necessarily inexplicable".[23] Scientism – the confidence that reality as such can be fully understood, articulated and explained by science alone – turns out to be hubris.

The sense of there being an ineffable "power", a *dao*, that is responsible for anything in nature figuring for us as it does must also militate against the tendency to regard nature as "our" world. The natural world, we saw in Chapter 7, is "other" than the human world of artefacts, "other" therefore than the product of us creatures who have "lost the Way". The concepts we apply to it have no more authority than those employed by creatures very different from ourselves, with different interests, sensory systems and so on. To recall Nietzsche's remark once more, there is hubris in supposing that the world presents itself to us, but not to gnats, as it really is.

If there is lack of humility in not recognizing the natural world as "other", it betrays an even greater lack if nature is then regarded as so much "equipment" – as a resource – for human beings to use as they please. What a sense of nature's mystery brings with it is the appreciation, by Heidegger and Wittgenstein, for example, that this technological, utilitarian perception is but one among many other ways that the natural world has presented itself to people. At one level, of course, everyone knows that nature cannot be simply a resource or pile of equipment. But it requires a sense of, an attunement to, the recessive, mysterious way of things if that knowledge is to translate into a way of regarding things with the "selfless respect" definitive, for Irish Murdoch, of humility.

Humility may also be understood, we've seen, as recognition of dependence on what people are wrongly tempted to regard as being of their own making, under their control. In religious traditions, this takes the form of recognition of one's dependence on the divine. For the Desert Fathers and St Benedict, for instance, humility in this form is a paramount virtue. It remains a virtue when the dependence that is acknowledged is upon something less theologically conceived – the *dao*, "One Life", or whatever. As we learned from the Buddha, human beings have a terrible tendency to exaggerate the extent of their mastery over their lives. In philosophy, the tendency is apparent in, for example, the Sartrean conceit that persons create themselves and their worlds from the ground up. The exaggeration here reflects and reinforces vanity, *amour-propre* and self-importance. The appreciation of a way of things that, so to speak, has destined one's talents, convictions and achievements excludes self-congratulation and invidious comparisons with others, inviting instead the exercise of equanimity and the eschewal of self-serving judgement.

Equanimity, compassion and related virtues are invited, too, by an aspect of the sense of mystery attested to by those who attempt to record this sense. This is the theme of the overall unity of reality. Wordsworth's is a sense of all things "deeply interfused"; Coleridge's is that of the "One Life"; the *dao* is said to "connect everything" together. So prominent is this theme that the urge to regard reality as a "unity" or undifferentiated "whole" has been held to be definitive of "nature-mysticism".[24]

Attested to, as well, by those who record a sense of the unity of all things is an extension of compassion and care to living beings. The recognition of unity and connection is sometimes taken, as by some Buddhists, to demonstrate that there are no individual selves or persons. But there is no need to accept this in order to appreciate how a sense of connection among all things – persons included – may instil compassion for other beings. I do not have to deny my individual, relatively enduring existence in order to care about the suffering of other individuals, all of whom, I now recognize, are in the same boat, as it were, as myself.[25]

Humility, equanimity, compassion and other quietist virtues are not, it's worth stressing, *entailed* by a doctrine of mystery. A logician may rightly question how one moves from a premise about the mystery and unity of nature to moral imperatives. But it misunderstands the relation between a sense of mystery and the quietist virtues to suppose that the former entails the latter. It's been rightly pointed out that the Buddha was not, in a good sense, engaged in moral philosophy at all – if, by this, we mean the attempt to *argue* for principles of right action. He was engaged, rather, in "moral phenomenology", the attempt to lucidly describe reality and get us to see it in a way that induces certain moral sensibilities.[26] The same could be said of Confucians, Daoists, Vedantists and many other ancient thinkers.

Once, for example, dependence on the way of things is internalized and attuned to, hubris will drop away. Again, with the lived, experiential recognition of the unity of all things, care for other beings naturally arises. In these and other cases, appreciation of reality dispels the perceptions, including self-perception, conducive to human failings – hubris, vanity, greed and the rest. They then wither away. Such, at least, is the hope of the moral phenomenologist.

In this chapter, the adequacy or completeness of the quietist response to disquiet – to pessimism and misanthropy – was questioned. The issue was whether the quietist life, supplemented by finding refuge in nature, is consonant with the way of things and hence "in the truth". Without some assurance that it is, the anxiety – itself destructive of quietist aspirations – will persist that this style of life is an indulgence, productive perhaps of contentment, but with no further warrant.

This warrant is provided, I've proposed, if one embraces the vision, recorded by poets and philosophers in many traditions, of the way of things as finally mysterious, resistant to conceptual articulation. If there is truth in this vision, then to live in a manner consonant with it is to be "in the truth". In two ways, we saw, the quietist life meets this criterion. Tranquillity, "not doing", patience and other quietist aspirations are pre-requisites for developing a sense of mystery, not least through removing obstacles to the arising of this sense. These aspir-ations, if achieved, cultivate a way of experiencing the world as the presencing of what is beyond articulation – the *dao*, *rta*, the "One Life", a rolling "spirit", a "mystic power", to cite a few of the stabs at giving this a name. Second, a sense of the mys-tery of things, once cultivated and secure, invites and fosters the exercise of quietist virtues – of humility, for example, or "selfless respect" for nature, and compassion.

It is in this double, circular movement – from the quietist style of life towards a sense of mystery, and from there back to virtues that belong to this style – that quietism receives warrant and enjoys the confidence of being "in the truth".

CODA

In "Tintern Abbey", Wordsworth refers to the "serene and blessed mood" that is experienced when "We see into the life of things". Heidegger writes of a sober "joy" that accompan-ies the understanding of the kind of being one is.[27] Buddhist texts speak of the "happiness and joy in this very life" that a bhikkhu derives from absorbing the truth of the Buddha's teaching.[28] Aristotle refers to "activity in accord with wis-dom" as "the most pleasant of the activities in accord with virtue".[29]

Here are just a few testimonies to an intimate connec-tion between truth and happiness. People feel happy – or joyful or blessed – when they are confident of having a sense of how things are, especially when this sense carries with it an intimation of how to live. The point applies to the sense

133

of mystery discussed over the preceding pages. It is reasonable, therefore, to hope that quietists might enjoy not only tranquillity, beauty, humaneness, refuge and an assurance of being "in the truth", but the happiness that comes with this assurance.

Does this hope contradict or expel the pessimism that was, after all, the starting point for quietist reflections and aspirations? No, for pessimism is essentially a negative verdict on the human condition that offers no prospect of any radical melioration of this condition. The quietist's hope, therefore, is not for a revolution that will bring an end to suffering and usher in an age of general happiness. But it is a hope that quietists might reasonably entertain for their own prospect of happiness, and for that of the people they may persuade, by word or example, of the wisdom of the quietist dispensation.

Notes

PROLOGUE

1. Annas, *The Morality of Happiness*, 3.
2. Burns, "Man was made to mourn – a dirge".

1. THE HUMAN CONDITION

1. Bodhi (ed.), *In the Buddha's Words*, 359–64.
2. *Ibid.*, 36.
3. *Ibid.*, 32, 346.
4. On the Buddha's pessimism and misanthropy, see Cooper, "Buddhism as pessimism".
5. Swift, "Letter to Pope". For recent discussions of pessimism and/or misanthropy, see Kidd, "Philosophical misanthropy"; Cooper, *Animals and Misanthropy*; Harris, *Misanthropy in the Age of Reason*; Gibson, *Misanthropy*; Beiser, *Weltschmerz*; and Dienstag, *Pessimism: Philosophy, Ethic, Spirit*.
6. See, for example, Bodhi (ed.), *In the Buddha's Words*, 356–7.
7. Sophocles, *Sophocles in English Verse*, 297.
8. Tertullian, *De Resurrectione Carnis*, 8–9.
9. Chadwick, Introduction to Saint Augustine, *Confessions*, xviii.
10. Johnston, *Saving God: Religion After Idolatry*, 173.
11. Rousseau, *Discourse on the Origin of Inequality*, 117.
12. Leopardi, *Thoughts*, 24 and 85.

13. Schopenhauer, *The World as Will and Representation* Vol. 2, 605.
14. Hartmann, *Philosophy of the Unconscious*, 130ff.
15. Cioran, *On the Heights of Despair*, 43.
16. Benatar, *Debating Procreation: Is It Wrong to Procreate?*, 111.
17. Ziporyn (tr.), *Zhuangzi: The Essential Writings*, ch. 12.
18. Quoted in The Dark Mountain Project, *Uncivilisation*, 1.
19. Ward (ed.), *The Desert Fathers: Sayings of the Early Christian Monks*, 11.
20. For persuasive criticism of "the achievement society", see Han, *The Burnout Society*.

2.   AMNESIA AND NIHILISM

1. Wittgenstein, *Tractatus Logico-Philosophicus*, §6.43.
2. *The Rule of St Benedict*, 22–3; Kierkegaard, *Concluding Unscientific Postscript*, 178.
3. Kant, *Lectures on Ethics*, 27: 672. On Kant on misanthropy, see Kidd, "Varieties of philosophical misanthropy".
4. McHarg, *Man: The Planetary Disease*, 1 and 3.
5. Patricia MacCormack, quoted in Kirsch, *The Revolt Against Humanity*, 43 – a useful survey of "anti-humanist" and "transhumanist" views.

3.   ACTIVISM

1. Rousseau, *Discourse*, 45; James, *On a Certain Blindness in Human Beings*, 35; Leopold, *A Sand County Almanac*, 262.
2. For a lively debate on this optimistic vision, see Pinker *et al.*, *Do Humankind's Best Days Lay Ahead?*
3. Huxley, *Island*, 86.
4. For these and other examples, see Chang, *23 Things They Don't Tell You About Capitalism*, 41ff.
5. Eliot, *Middlemarch*, 688.
6. Walshe (tr.), *The Long Discourses of the Buddha*, No. 26.
7. Ivanhoe (tr.), *The Daodejing of Laozi*, ch. 60.
8. Epicurus, *The Epicurus Reader*, 39; *Zhuangzi*, ch. 7; Augustine, *The City of God*, §19.17; Walshe (tr.), *The Long Discourses*, No. 26.

9. Augustine, *Confessions*, 47.
10. Huxley, *Island*, 152.
11. *Daodejing*, chs. 19 and 66.
12. For criticism of "activist" interpretations of the Buddha's views, see Kidd, "Should Buddhists be social activists?".
13. Epicurus, *The Epicurus Reader*, 80; Walshe (tr.), *The Long Discourses*, No. 26; Augustine, *An Augustine Synthesis*, 268–9.
14. Kingsnorth, "Confessions of a recovering environmentalist", 4 and 12.
15. Franzen, *What If We Stopped Pretending?*, 47.
16. Kingsnorth, "Confessions", 13.
17. Quoted in Norlock, "Perpetual struggle", 3; Norlock offers a nuanced defence of Leopold's view.
18. Tessman, "Expecting bad luck", 9–10.

4. QUIETISM

1. See al-Sarhan (ed.), *Political Quietism in Islam*.
2. Schopenhauer, *World as Will and Representation* Vol. 1, 385.
3. The following quotes are from a nineteenth-century compilation of remarks by Molinos, Guyon and Archbishop Fénelon, *A Guide to True Peace*, 23, 28, 54–5, 57 and 73.
4. Fénelon, *Maxims of the Saints*, articles 2 and 3.
5. *The Desert Fathers*, 11.
6. See Magee, "Quietism in German mysticism".
7. Wittgenstein, *Tractatus*, §4.112.
8. Wittgenstein, *Philosophical Investigations*, §§124, 133 and 255.
9. Wittgenstein, *On Certainty*, §§341–3.
10. Montaigne, *The Complete Essays*, 204 and 629.
11. Wittgenstein, *Philosophical Investigations*, §127.
12. *Zhuangzi*, ch. 4.
13. *Daodejing*, ch. 67.
14. *Zhuangzi*, ch. 5.
15. *The Epicurus Reader*, 29.
16. Epictetus, *The Enchyridion and Discourses of Epictetus*, §1.
17. See Hadot, *Philosophy as a Way of Life*.
18. See Foot, *Natural Goodness*, ch. 1.

19. Aristotle, *Nicomachean Ethics*, Bk 1, §13.
20. *Ibid.*, Bk 2, §§4ff.

5.   MODES OF QUIETISM

1. Bodhi (tr.), *The Connected Discourses of the Buddha*, 47.19.
2. Kant, *Lectures on Ethics*, 672.
3. Leary, *Turn On, Tune In, Drop Out*, 3.
4. Jerry Garcia, quoted in Rorabaugh, *American Hippies*, 65.
5. Leary, *Turn On*, 87–8.
6. A good discussion of *wu wei* is Slingerland, *Trying Not to Try*.
7. *Zhuangzi*, ch. 19.
8. *Daodejing*, ch. 48.
9. On irony and Daoism, see Moeller and D'Ambrosio, *Genuine Pretending: On the Philosophy of the Zhuangzi*.
10. Møllgaard, *An Introduction to Daoist Thought*, 17.
11. *Zhuangzi*, 24.
12. Heidegger, *The Question Concerning Technology*, 33.
13. Quoted in Thompson, "Quietism for the sake of happiness", 406.
14. Alberti, *On Painting*, 18.
15. *Zhuangzi*, ch. 19.
16. Kierkegaard, *The Sickness Unto Death*, excerpted in Bretall (ed.), *A Kierkegaard Anthology*, 341 and 357.

6.   REFUGE

1. Montaigne, *The Complete Essays*, 270.
2. Pascal, *Pensées*, §168.
3. Sebald, *Austerlitz*, 213.
4. Huxley, *The Doors of Perception and Heaven and Hell*, 38.
5. Ambrose, *Treatise on Flight from the World*.
6. Nyanaponika, *The Vision of Dhamma*, 232.
7. See Cooper, "The rhetoric of refuge".
8. Montaigne, *The Complete Essays*, 270.
9. Quoted in Zweig, *The World of Yesterday*, 23.
10. Wordsworth, "The World Is Too Much With Us".
11. Leopardi, *Thoughts*, §89.

12. *Zhuangzi*, ch. 26. The point made in this paragraph was suggested to me by John Shand.
13. See Jamison, *Finding Sanctuary*.
14. Sartre, *Nausea*, 37–9.

7.   NATURE AS REFUGE 1: "ANOTHER PLACE"

1. Thoreau, *Walden*, 382.
2. Abbey, *Confessions of a Barbarian*, 158.
3. Sebald, *The Emigrants*, 22 and 110.
4. Wang Wei, in Harris (tr.), *300 Hundred Tang Poems*, 224.
5. Norman (tr.), *The Elders' Verses* Vol. 1, vv. 13, 14, 35, 523, 601 and 1135–6.
6. Kamo-no-Chomei, *Hojoki*; Shiwu in Red Pine (tr.), *The Mountain Poems of Stonehouse*, 25 and 155.
7. Heidegger, "Messkirch's Seventh Centennial", 44.
8. Merton, *Raids on the Unspeakable*, 8.
9. See Kidd, "Gardens of refuge".
10. Ryōkan, *One Robe, One Bowl: The Zen Poetry of Ryōkan*, 48.
11. Church, *Gardens Are For People*, 6.
12. See Jones, *Losing Eden: Why Our Minds Need The Wild*, Part 3.
13. Fowles, cited in Mabey, *Nature Cure*, 148.
14. Merton, *When The Trees Say Nothing*, 44.
15. Sartre, *Nausea*, 183–6.
16. On aesthetic experiences of nature versus those of artworks, see Berleant, *The Aesthetics of Environment*.
17. Thoreau, *Walden*, 563.
18. Don Maier, quoted in James, *How Nature Matters*, 116 – a book very pertinent to the present discussion.
19. Nietzsche, *Philosophy and Truth*, 79.
20. Thoreau, *Walden*, 557.
21. Adams, *Gardens Through History*, 319.
22. Macfarlane, *The Wild Places*, 32.
23. Schopenhauer, *The World as Will and Representation*, Vol. 2, 404; for a discussion of his and related views, see Cooper, *A Philosophy of Gardens*, ch. 5.
24. Graham (tr.), *The Book of Lieh-Tzu*, ch. 2.

8.   NATURE AS REFUGE 2: "A BETTER PLACE"

1. Thoreau, *Walden*, 389.
2. Schiller, "On naïve and sentimental poetry", 181–2.
3. Hale, *The Wild and the Wicked*, 3.
4. Dillard, *Pilgrim At Tinker's Creek*, 9, 66 and 170.
5. Hale, *The Wild and the Wicked*, 94–5.
6. Lorenz, *King Solomon's Ring*, 106–107.
7. I argue for this asymmetry in *Animals and Misanthropy*, ch. 5.
8. Kant, *Critique of Judgement*, Part 1, §42.
9. *Ibid.*
10. *Ibid.*
11. *Zhuangzi*, ch. 14.
12. Schiller, "On naïve and sentimental poetry", 184 and 187.
13. *Elders' Verses*, v. 717.
14. Murdoch, *The Sovereignty of the Good*, 369.
15. Rousseau, *Reveries of a Solitary Walker*, 91.
16. Murdoch, *The Sovereignty of the Good*, 369–70.
17. Schiller, "On naïve and sentimental poetry", 181.
18. Kierkegaard, *The Lily of the Field and the Bird of the Air*, 5.
19. Murdoch, *The Sovereignty of the Good*, 370.
20. See Saito, *Aesthetics of Care*, 124; a book that furnishes many examples of the relation between beauty and virtue.
21. Kant, *Critique of Judgement*, Part 1, §42.
22. *Ibid.*
23. Yuanming, "Returning to live in the country", 54.
24. Thoreau, "Walking", 592.
25. *Zhuangzi*, ch. 26; Bashō, *The Narrow Road to the Deep North*, 85; Rousseau, *Reveries*, 91.
26. Sartre, *Being and Nothingness*, 15.
27. Baker, *The Peregrine*, 178.
28. *Zhuangzi*, chs. 6 and 18.
29. Jeffers, "The inhumanist", 304.
30. Schiller, "On naïve and sentimental poetry", 182.
31. *Daodejing*, ch. 25.
32. Graham, *Chuang-Tzu: The Inner Chapters*, 14.

33. Muir, "Our National Parks", quoted in Jones, *Why Our Minds Need the Wild*, 37.
34. Thoreau, "Walking", 592.
35. Knausgaard, *The Morning Star*, 385–6.
36. See Wilson, *Biophilia*.
37. Rilke, *Rilke's Late Poetry*, 46–7.
38. Heidegger, *Being and Time*, 236.

9. QUIETISM, TRUTH AND MYSTERY

1. "Lines composed above Tintern Abbey".
2. Hepburn, "Landscape and the metaphysical imagination", 191.
3. Kierkegaard, *Christian Discourses*, 328.
4. Lorenzatos, *Aegean Notebooks*, 111.
5. Thoreau, "Walking", 625.
6. Coleridge, "Frost at Midnight" and "The Eolian Harp".
7. Johnston, *Saving God: Religion After Idolatry*, 158.
8. Mahler, quoted in Franklin, *The Life of Mahler*, 99.
9. Bergson, *The Two Sources of Morality and Religion*, 180–82.
10. On *rta*, *qi* and related notions, see Armstrong, *Sacred Nature*, ch. 2.
11. *Zhuangzi*, ch. 22.
12. *Daodejing*, ch. 1.
13. Kierkegaard, *Christian Discourses*, 329.
14. Hepburn, "Landscape and the metaphysical imagination", 191, and "Aesthetic appreciation of nature", 199 and 206.
15. *Daodejing*, chs. 41 and 77.
16. Mahler, quoted in Lebrecht, *Mahler Remembered*, 172.
17. Kierkegaard, *The Sickness Unto Death*, 341–3.
18. Tolstoy, *A Confession and Other Religious Writings*, 77.
19. *Zhuangzi*, ch. 2.
20. Tolstoy, *A Confession*, 141.
21. Fronsdal (tr.), *The Dhammapada*, vv. 356, 362 and 378.
22. See Cooper, *Senses of Mystery* for a defence of this view.
23. Tolstoy, *A Confession*, 78.
24. See, for example, Hepburn, "Aesthetic appreciation of nature", 206.

25. See McGhee, *Spirituality for the Godless*, 167–8.
26. On the Buddha as a moral phenomenologist, see Garfield, *Buddhist Ethics*, ch. 3.
27. Heidegger, *Being and Time*, 358.
28. Bodhi (tr.), *The Numerical Discourses of the Buddha*, Bk. 6, §78.
29. Aristotle, *Nicomachean Ethics*, Bk 9, §7.

References

Abbey, E. *Confessions of a Barbarian: Selections from the Journals of Edward Abbey, 1951–89*. London: Little Brown, 1994.

Abram, D. *Becoming Animal: An Earthly Cosmology*. New York: Vintage, 2011.

Adams, W. H. *Gardens Through History: Nature Perfected*. New York: Abbeville, 1991.

Alberti, L. B. *On Painting*. New Haven, CT: Yale University Press, 1970.

Al-Sarhan, S. (ed.). *Political Quietism in Islam: Sunni and Shi'i Practice and Thought*. London: I. B. Tauris, 2020.

Ambrose, St. *Treatise on Flight from the World*. Available at https://www.catholic.org/lent/story.php?id=32593.

Annas, J. *The Morality of Happiness*. Oxford: Oxford University Press, 1993.

Aristotle. *Nicomachean Ethics*. Indianapolis, IN: Hackett, 1999.

Armstrong, K. *Sacred Nature: How We Can Recover Our Bond With The Natural World*. London: Penguin, 2022.

Augustine, St. *An Augustine Synthesis*. London: Sheed & Ward, 1936.

Augustine, St. *Confessions*. Oxford: Oxford University Press, 1998.

Augustine, St. *The City of God*. London: Penguin, 2003.

Backhouse, W. & J. Janson (eds). *A Guide to True Peace: The 1815 Edition*. CreateSpace, 2015.

Baker, J. A. *The Peregrine*. New York: New York Review of Books, 2005.

Bashō, M. *The Narrow Road to the Deep North and Other Travel Sketches*. London: Penguin, 1966.

Beiser, F. *Weltschmerz: Pessimism in German Philosophy 1860–1900*. Oxford: Oxford University Press, 2018.

Benatar, D. & D. Wasserman. *Debating Procreation: Is It Wrong To Procreate?* Oxford: Oxford University Press, 2015.

Benedict, St. *The Rule of St Benedict.* London: Penguin, 2008.

Bergson, H. *The Two Sources of Morality and Religion.* London: Macmillan, 1935.

Berleant, A. *The Aesthetics of Environment.* Philadelphia, PA: Temple University Press, 1992.

Bodhi, Bhikkhu (tr.). *The Connected Discourses of the Buddha.* Somerville, MA: Wisdom Publications, 2000.

Bodhi, Bhikkhu (ed.). *In the Buddha's Words: An Anthology of Discourses from the Pāli Canon.* Somerville, MA: Wisdom Publications, 2005.

Bodhi, Bhikkhu (tr.). *The Numerical Discourses of the Buddha.* Somerville, MA: Wisdom Publications, 2012.

Burns, R. "Man was made to mourn – a dirge". Available at https://www.poetryverse.com/robert-burns-poems/made-mourn.

Chang, H.-J. *23 Things They Don't Tell You About Capitalism.* London: Penguin, 2011.

Church, T. *Gardens Are For People.* Berkeley, CA: University of California Press, 1995.

Cioran, E. *On the Heights of Despair.* Chicago, IL: University of Chicago Press, 1992.

Coleridge, S. T. "Frost at midnight". Available at https://www.poetryfoundation.org/poems/43986.

Coleridge, S. T. "The Eolian Harp". Available at https://www.poetryfoundation.org/poems/52301.

Cooper, D. E. *A Philosophy of Gardens.* Oxford: Oxford University Press, 2006.

Cooper, D. E. *Animals and Misanthropy.* London: Routledge, 2018.

Cooper, D. E. *Senses of Mystery: Engaging with Nature and the Meaning of Life.* London: Routledge, 2018.

Cooper, D. E. "Buddhism as pessimism". *Journal of World Philosophies* 6 (2021), 1–16.

Cooper, D. E. "The rhetoric of refuge". *Daily Philosophy* 2021. Available at https://daily-philosophy.com/cooper-rhetoric-of-refuge.

Dark Mountain Project, The. *Uncivilisation: The Dark Mountain Manifesto.* Padstow: The Dark Mountain Project, 2019.

Dienstag, J. F. *Pessimism: Philosophy, Ethic, Spirit.* Princeton, NJ: Princeton University Press, 2006.

Dillard, A. *Pilgrim at Tinker's Creek.* New York: HarperCollins, 2007.

Eliot, G. *Middlemarch.* London: Wordsworth Editions, 1993.

Epicurus. *The Epicurus Reader*. Indianapolis, IN: Hackett, 1994.

Epictetus. *The Enchiridion and Discourses of Epictetus*. CreateSpace, 2018.

Fénelon, F. *Maxims of the Saints from François Fénelon*. CreateSpace, 2018.

Foot, P. *Natural Goodness*. Oxford: Oxford University Press, 2003.

Franklin, P. *The Life of Mahler*. Cambridge: Cambridge University Press, 1997.

Franzen, J. *What If We Stopped Pretending?* London: Fourth Estate, 2021.

Fronsdal, G. (tr.). *The Dhammapada*. Boston, MA: Shambhala, 2006.

Garfield, J. *Buddhist Ethics: A Philosophical Exploration*. Oxford: Oxford University Press, 2022.

Gibson, A. *Misanthropy: The Critique of Humanity*. London: Bloomsbury, 2017.

Graham, A. C. (tr.). *The Book of Lieh-Tzu: A Classic of the Tao*. New York: Columbia University Press, 1990.

Graham, A. C. (tr.). *Chuang-Tzu: The Inner Chapters*. Indianapolis, IN: Hackett, 2001.

Hadot, P. *Philosophy as a Way of Life*. Oxford: Blackwell, 1995.

Hale, B. *The Wild and the Wicked: On Nature and Human Nature*. Cambridge, MA: MIT Press, 2016.

Han, B.-C. *The Burnout Society*. Stanford, CA: Stanford University Press, 2015.

Harris, J. *Misanthropy in the Age of Reason: Hating Humanity from Shakespeare to Schiller*. Oxford: Oxford University Press, 2022.

Harris, P. (tr.). *300 Tang Poems*. London: Everyman, 2009.

Hartmann, E. *Philosophy of the Unconscious*, London: Kegan Paul, Trench & Trübner, 1893.

Heidegger, M. "Messkirch's Seventh Centennial". *Listening: Journal of Religion and Culture* 1–3 (1973), 40–57.

Heidegger, M. *The Question Concerning Technology and Other Essays*. New York: Harper & Row, 1977.

Heidegger, M. *Being and Time*. Oxford: Blackwell, 1980.

Hepburn, R. W. "Aesthetic appreciation of nature". *British Journal of Aesthetics* 3 (1963), 195–209.

Hepburn, R. W. "Landscape and the metaphysical imagination". *Environmental Values* 5 (1996), 191–204.

Huxley, A. *The Doors of Perception* and *Heaven and Hell*. London: Vintage, 2004.

Huxley, A. *Island*. London: Vintage, 2005.

Ivanhoe, P. (tr.). *The Daodejing of Laozi*. Indianapolis, IN: Hackett, 2002.

James, S. P. *How Nature Matters*. Oxford: Oxford University Press, 2022.

James, W. *On a Certain Blindness in Human Beings*. London: Penguin, 2009.

Jamison, C. *Finding Sanctuary: Monastic Steps for Everyday Life*. London: Orion, 2006.

Jeffers, R. "The inhumanist". In *The Collected Poetry of Robinson Jeffers*, Vol. 3. Stanford, CA: Stanford University Press, 1991.

Johnston, M. *Saving God: Religion after Idolatry*. Princeton, NJ: Princeton University Press, 2009.

Jones, L. *Losing Eden: Why Our Minds Need the Wild*. London: Penguin, 2020.

Kano-no-Chomei. *Hojoki: Visions of a Torn World*. Berkeley, CA: Stonebridge, 1996.

Kant, I. *Critique of Judgement*. Oxford: Oxford University Press, 1952.

Kant, I. *Lectures on Ethics*. Cambridge: Cambridge University Press, 1997.

Kidd, I. J. "Philosophical misanthropy". *Philosophy Now*, Aug/Sept 2020, 22–5.

Kidd, I. J. "Gardens of refuge". *Daily Philosophy*, Oct 2021.

Kidd, I. J. "Varieties of philosophical misanthropy". *Journal of Philosophical Research* 46 (2021), 27–44.

Kidd, I. J. "Should Buddhists be social activists?". *Daily Philosophy*, 2022. Available at https://daily-philosophy.com/kidd-buddhism-social-activism-part-1/.

Kierkegaard, S. *The Sickness Unto Death*. Excerpted in R. Bretall (ed.), *A Kierkegaard Anthology*. Princeton, NJ: Princeton University Press, 1973.

Kierkegaard, S. *Christian Discourses*. Excerpted in H. & E. Hong (eds.), *The Essential Kierkegaard*. Princeton, NJ: Princeton University Press, 2000.

Kierkegaard, S. *The Lily of the Field and the Bird of the Air: The Godly Discourses*. Princeton, NJ: Princeton University Press, 2018.

Kingsnorth, P. "Confessions of a recovering environmentalist". 2010. Available at https://paulkingsnorth.net/confessions.

Kirsch, A. *The Revolt Against Humanity: Imagining a Future Without Us*. New York: Columbia Global Reports, 2023.

Knausgaard, K. O. *The Morning Star*. London: Vintage, 2021.

Leary, T. *Turn On, Tune In, Drop Out*. Oakland, CA: Ronin, 1999.

Lebrecht, N. *Mahler Remembered*. London: Faber & Faber, 2010.

Leopardi, G. *Thoughts*. London: Hesperus, 2002.

Leopold, A. *A Sand County Almanac*. New York: Ballantyne, 1970.

Lorenz, K. *King Solomon's Ring*. London: Methuen, 1961.

Lorenzatos, Z. *Aegean Notebooks*. Limni, Greece: Denise Harvey, 2016.

Mabey, R. *Nature Cure*. London: Chatto & Windus, 2005.

Macfarlane, R. *The Wild Places*. London: Granta, 2007.

McGhee, M. *Spirituality for the Godless: Buddhism, Humanism, and Religion*. Cambridge: Cambridge University Press, 2021.

McHarg, I. *Man: The Planetary Disease*. Washington, DC: Agriculture Research Service, 1971.

Magee, G. A. "Quietism in German philosophy and mysticism". *Common Knowledge* 16 (2010), 457–73.

Marvell, A. "Thoughts in a Garden". Available at https://poetryfoundation.org/poems/44682.

Merton, T. *Raids on the Unspeakable*. London: Burns & Oates, 1977.

Merton, T. *When the Trees Say Nothing: Writings on Nature*. Notre Dame, IL: Sorin, 2003.

Moeller, H.-G. & P. D'Ambrosio. *Genuine Pretending: On the Philosophy of the* Zhuangzi. New York: Columbia University Press, 2017.

Møllgaard, E. *An Introduction to Daoist Thought*. London: Routledge, 2011.

Montaigne, M. *The Complete Essays*. London: Penguin, 1991.

Murdoch, I. "The sovereignty of the good". In I. Murdoch, *Existentialists and Mystics: Writings on Philosophy and Literature*. London: Penguin, 1999.

Nietzsche, F. *Philosophy and Truth: Selections from Nietzsche's Notebooks of the Early 1870s*. Atlantic Highlands, NJ: Humanities Press.

Norlock, K. J. "Perpetual struggle". *Hypatia* 34 (2018), 6–19.

Norman, K. (tr.), *Elders' Verses: I Theragāthā*. Lancaster: Pali Text Society, 2007.

Nyanaponika. *The Vision of Dhamma: Buddhist Writings of Nyanaponika Thera*. Kandy: Buddhist Publication Society, 1994.

Pascal, B. *Pensées*. Oxford: Oxford University Press, 1995.

Pine, R. (tr.). *The Mountain Poems of Stonehouse*. Port Townsend, WA: Copper Canyon Press, 2014.

Pinker, S. *et al. Do Humankind's Best Days Lie Ahead? Munk Debate*. London: Oneworld, 2016.

Rilke, R. M. *Rilke's Late Poetry*. Tr. G. Good. Vancouver: Ronsdale, 2004.

Rorabaugh, W. J. *American Hippies*. Cambridge: Cambridge University Press, 2015.

Rousseau, J.-J. *Reveries of a Solitary Walker*. Indianapolis, IN: Hackett, 1992.

Rousseau, J.-J. *Discourse on the Origin of Inequality*. Oxford: Oxford University Press, 1994.

Ryōkan. *One Robe, One Bowl: The Zen Poetry of Ryōkan*. Tr. J. Stevens. Boston, MA: Weatherhill, 2006.

Saito, Y. *Aesthetics of Care*. London: Bloomsbury, 2022.

Sartre, J.-P. *Being and Nothingness: An Essay in Phenomenological Ontology*. London: Methuen, 1957.

Sartre, J.-P. *Nausea*. London: Penguin, 1965.

Schiller, F. "On naïve and sentimental poetry". In F. Schiller, *Essays*, 179–260. New York: Continuum, 2001.

Schopenhauer, A. *The World as Will and Representation*. 2 vols. New York: Dover, 1969.

Sebald, W. G. *The Emigrants*. London: Vintage, 1996.

Sebald, W. G. *Austerlitz*. London: Penguin, 2002.

Slingerland, E. *Trying Not to Try*. Edinburgh: Canongate, 2014.

Sophocles, *Oedipus at Colona*. In *Sophocles: The Seven Plays in English Verse*, 259–312. Tr. L. Campbell. Oxford: Oxford University Press, 1949.

Swift, J. "Letter to Alexander Pope 29th Sept 1725". Available at https://www.ourcivilisation.com/smartboard/shop/swift/letters/chap2.htm.

Tao Yuanming. "Returning to live in the country". In *Tao Yuanming: The Complete Works*, 54–7. Tr. E. Trotter. Chatham, ON: Peach Blossom Press, 2022.

Tennyson, A. "The Lotos-Eaters". Available at https://www.poetryfoundation.org/poems/45364.

Tertullian. *De Resurrectione Carnis*. Available at https://www.vatican.va/spirit/documents/spirit_20000908_tertulliano_en.html.

Tessman, L. "Expecting bad luck". *Hypatia* 24 (2009), 9–28.

Thompson, C. "Quietism from the side of happiness: Tolstoy, Schopenhauer, War and Peace". *Common Knowledge* 15 (2009), 395–411.

Thoreau, H. D. *Walden*. In *The Portable Thoreau*, 253–572. London: Penguin, 1977.

Thoreau, H. D. "Walking". In *The Portable Thoreau*, 592–630. London: Penguin, 1977.

Tolstoy, L. *A Confession and Other Religious Writings*. London: Penguin, 1987.

Walshe, M. (tr.). *The Long Discourses of the Buddha*. Boston, MA: Wisdom Publications, 1995.

Ward, B. *The Desert Fathers: Sayings of the Early Christian Monks*. London: Penguin, 2003.

Wilson, E. O. *Biophilia*. Cambridge, MA: Harvard University Press, 1984.

Wittgenstein, L. *Philosophical Investigations*. Oxford: Blackwell, 1968.

Wittgenstein, L. *On Certainty*. Oxford: Blackwell, 1969.

Wittgenstein, L. *Tractatus Logico-Philosophicus*. London: Routledge, 1974.

Wordsworth, W. "The world is too much with us". Available at https://www.poetryfoundation.org/poems/45564.

Wordsworth, W. "Lines composed above Tintern Abbey on revisiting the banks of the Wye during a tour, July 13th 1798". Available at https://www.poetryfoundation.org/poems/45527.

Ziporyn, B. (tr.). *Zhuangzi: The Essential Writings*. Indianapolis, IN: Hackett, 2009.

Zweig, S. *The World of Yesterday*. London: Pushkin Press, 2010.

Index